In and Out of the Black Box

In and Out of the Black Box

On the Philosophy of Cognition

D. W. HAMLYN

Basil Blackwell

First published 1990

Basil Blackwell Ltd
108 Cowley Road, Oxford OX4 1JF, UK

Basil Blackwell, Inc.
3 Cambridge Center
Cambridge, Massachusetts 02142, USA

British Library Cataloguing in Publication Data

A CIP catalogue record for this book is available from the British Library

Library of Congress Cataloguing in Publication Data

Hamlyn, D.W., 1924–
    In and out of the black box: on the philosophy of cognition / D.W.
Hamlyn.
        p.   cm.
    Bibliography: p.
    Includes index.
    ISBN 0–631–15757–3
    1. Cognitive psychology—Philosophy.   2. Cognition.   I. Title.
II. Title: Philosophy of cognition.
BF311.H315   1990   89–34519
153—dc20   CIP

Typeset in Times 11 on 12.5 pt
by Vera-Reyes, Inc.
Printed in Great Britain by TJ Press Ltd., Padstow, Cornwall

Contents

Preface

Although I have had a book of this kind in mind for some time, and especially since the publication of my *Perception, Learning and the Self*, I was somewhat nervous about embarking on it, in the light of the complexity and technicality of some of the issues. I was pushed in its direction to some extent by Kim Pickin when she worked for Basil Blackwell. I am grateful to her for her encouragement, as I am for that of Stephan Chambers, her successor at Basil Blackwell. But I am especially grateful for all the pressure that was put on me by my colleague Martin Davies, who simply assumed that I would indeed write it. He has, additionally, read the typescript and made innumerable helpful comments. I am sure that he does not agree with all that I have said, but his help and encouragement all the same have been invaluable.

Other colleagues have made helpful comments on earlier presentations of some of the material. I have also presented some of the issues in lectures to students at Birkbeck College, who like all previous generations of such students have been marvellous in their response. Since my retirement from the Chair of Philosophy at Birkbeck College these students, and colleagues also, are all, I suppose, 'ex-'. But they will always be with me in one way or another. I am deeply grateful to them and to Birkbeck, wonderful institution that it is.

Introduction

Cognitive psychology is a comparatively new branch of the subject. Thirty years ago it did not exist. To say that is not to deny that at and before that time psychology studied cognitive processes such as perception, memory and thinking. Historically, indeed, and looking further back, the study of such things was what the study of the mind was thought to be. Whether psychologists at the time would have considered that in studying such processes they were concerned with cognition is another matter. The term, after all, is something of a full-blown one; it gives a certain dignity to the processes to which it is given application. Nevertheless, perception, memory and thinking seem, on the face of it, admirably suitable subjects for psychology to be concerned with. In this country F. C. Bartlett's *Remembering* was regarded as something of a seminal text.[1] On the continent of Europe the Gestalt Psychologists were very much concerned with the subject of perception, and indeed with aspects of thinking also. None of this, however, delimited an approach to psychology which was to be given the title of Cognitive Psychology; it was simply psychology.

In this respect behaviourism was different in that it involved, *prima facie*, a doctrine about the subject-matter of psychology, which prescribed and laid down the frontiers and the territory of the subject. According to it the subject-matter of psychology was behaviour. It does not matter for present purposes that, as I shall try to show later, the notion of behaviour was underdetermined. Officially, the subject-matter of psychology was laid down by behaviourism in such a way that the sort of cognitive processes which I have mentioned above had little, if any, part to play in it. Psychology was concerned simply with behaviour and with such modifications of behaviour as could plausibly be brought under the heading of learning. Cognitive psychology, as it exists at present, was born, in effect, out of a dissatisfaction with behaviourism, partly for theoretical reasons and partly because of a belief that behaviourism had little to show in the way of success. As a replacement for behaviourism, however, it inherited much of its general character as an attempt to delimit the subject-matter of psychology, and arguably it also inherited some of its defects. That it did the latter is very much the thesis of this book.

There is one further point in this connection. In its reaction to behaviourism, cognitive psychology has laid weight upon what are usually called central processes. The general materialist attitudes which have become prevalent, and the natural concern that psychology should be seen by all as a science, have produced the belief that the central processes in question should be regarded either as neurological processes or as systems of processes identified simply in terms of their function but such that their realization is likely to be physiological in some way. The advent of and emphasis upon computers has also led quite naturally to the belief that these so-called central processes must function in a computational way, relying on data provided by the input through the senses. Perception, therefore, is to be thought of, on this account, in terms of the input of information. Once the computational processes have taken place there will, subject to the satisfaction of certain other conditions, be an output of some kind. This will be what behaviour consists in. The picture which all this presents, the conglomeration of cognitive psychology, physiology, computational theory, and in that sense artificial intelligence, is what has become known as cognitive science. If what is said above is true, that cognitive psychology has inherited some of the defects of behaviourism, the same must be true of the conglomeration of which cognitive psychology is a part, that is to say of cognitive science.

The position with regard to behaviourism might be stated as follows. B. F. Skinner, who came to be regarded as the high priest of behaviourism, once said that the letters 'CNS', normally taken as meaning 'Central Nervous System', should really be taken as meaning 'Conceptual Nervous System'. In saying this, he was signalling both his opposition to a consideration of anything lying inside an organism when attempting to explain its behaviour and his belief that we do not know enough, and are not likely to know enough, about physiology to make reference to it at all profitable in this connection. On this view, the organism, it is commonly said, is like a black box (black because we cannot see inside it and should therefore not attempt to do so); in explaining the behaviour of an organism we should confine our attention to input and output. In behaviourist terms the relation between input and output is that between stimulus and response. Indeed, to put the matter in terms of input and output is really to construe the behaviourist theoretical framework in terms of a quite different theoretical apparatus, that of information processing; but there is no harm in doing that so long as we recognize that that is what we are doing. Behaviourism, therefore, may justifiably be thought of as a black box theory according to which output from the box is to be explained, if at all, only by reference to its connection with output.

By contrast, any centralist theory seeks to go inside the box and explain the connection between input and output by reference to events or processes which take place inside it. In so far as this is simply a reaction to behaviourism such a theory will not challenge the conceptions of input and output which behaviourism has embraced. It will maintain only that concentration on input and output alone is unprofitable, because such connections as exist between the two cannot be explained entirely in their terms. To attempt to do so will clearly be a mistake if the conceptions of input and output which are employed are themselves flawed. In any assessment of cognitive psychology and cognitive science, therefore, it must be important first to get clear about the conceptions of input and output which are presupposed. It might be objected to this that it must be true on any account that the organism receives information from its environment and responds to it. Why cannot we, therefore, go direct to a theory of information processing and ask simply what is necessary if that is to be possible? The answer to that question is that we are surely concerned with *psychology*. In the end, the theory has to have something to do with what people and animals do and with what makes it possible for them to do it. We are not concerned simply with the properties of information-processing systems as such; at best these are supposed to provide a model for the construal of human and animal behaviour. The model is a model, and however interesting it is it is not being studied solely for its own sake.

My aim in what follows, therefore, is twofold. First, it is to answer the question what sort of thing, given a proper conception of input and output in the case of human and animal organisms, is to be thought of as intervening between input and output in such a way as to explain such connections between them as exist. But, second, it is to arrive at that proper conception of input and output, without which no understanding of what intervenes could be adequate. For if we content ourselves with the thought that there must, on any account, be input and output, and that it does not matter much how these are construed, the theory that is then constructed may have no relevance to an understanding of human and animal behaviour. That, in effect, is one major criticism that has been made of behaviourism itself, or at all events it is a major criticism that can be made of it, once the inadequacies of its construal of input and output in terms of stimulus and response are recognized. Hence, a critical examination of behaviourism is not a case of flogging a dead horse. In getting clear about behaviourism we *ipso facto* clarify the conceptual framework of those theories which have reacted to it by going inside the black box but otherwise simply adding more details of the same kind of thing.

I have made reference to behaviour several times in what I have said up to this point. One does not have to accept behaviourism in order to accept that in being concerned with psychology we must be concerned with what human beings and animals do; and that is to be concerned with their behaviour. That, in some sense, is what output must amount to in any theory which is *psychologically* relevant. On the input side it seems equally evident that from a psychological point of view input amounts to perception. Putting the matter in the most basic terms, animals and human beings behave as they do in part at least because they perceive in certain ways what is around them. It tends to be the conventional wisdom among contemporary philosophers that in explaining behaviour we make reference to some complex of beliefs and desires. When people do something it is because they want something and believe that such and such behaviour is necessary to achieve that end; or, they want something and perceive that such and such is relevant to the achievement of that end. It is doubtful whether that prototype for the explanation of behaviour is always adequate for its purpose (and I shall return to some issues which relate to that in a later chapter). What is more important for present purposes is the terms in which the thesis is expressed. It is often said that terms such as 'behaviour', 'belief' and 'perception' are terms which belong to 'folk psychology', the psychology of everyday life, and when that is said it is often in terms of disparagement, with the implication that if we cling to folk psychology we cling to the psychology of the stone age. Scientific psychology, it is said, knows better.

Surely, however, psychology, whether scientific or not, must have some relevance to human beings and animals as such; it must not be concerned merely with organisms, machines or abstract systems. We have a reasonably adequate everyday understanding of people. So-called folk psychology, whatever its status, constitutes in consequence the bench-mark by reference to which any theory must be judged if it is to be assessed as psychology. In its terms it is not enough to construe input and output simply as stimulus and response or in any terms which do not do justice to what behaviour, construed as action, and perception are. Hence, if I am asked what, given input and output, is to be taken as an adequate account of what is inside the black box, I shall be tempted to reply that if input and output do not amount to perception and action respectively no account of the kind in question will do. There may be physical, physiological and other processes which make perception and action possible, and which are in that sense part of the input and output, but that does not undermine my point.

It might be objected to this that to insist on the theory's conformity with a conception of psychology which has folk psychology as its basis is to take a too circumscribed view of what needs to be accounted for. Why cannot one simply bypass all these considerations about how input and output are to be construed in order to provide a connection with our ordinary ways of explaining people's behaviour, and go directly towards an account which interprets a human being as a biological or even physical system? Then input and output will, likewise, be construable in biological or physical terms. If this line is taken, the first thing to note must be the immense complexity of the situation so conceived. In the case of the higher organisms at least, the relation between the physical input to the organism construed as a physical system and any subsequent output of a similar kind must be so complex as to be almost mind-boggling. The situation is little better if one thinks of it in biological terms. In any case, the aim should not merely be that of providing adequate predictions; it must also be to provide an adequate understanding of what is going on. What is inevitably missing from any theory of the kinds contemplated is the provision of any understanding of people as people. To say that it would not then be psychology is not just an empty phrase; it is to say that something very important is left out when people and animals are treated merely as physical or biological systems.

In saying that, I do not mean to take up a question-begging position on the mind–body problem, suggesting that what is left out of the other theories is any reference to the mental, however that is to be understood. Whether psycho-physical dualism is true or false is in part a matter of fact and partly a matter of how the terms in which the issue is expressed are to be understood. The thought that something is left out when people and animals are treated simply as physical or biological systems may or may not presuppose a position on the question of dualism. That is not something into which it is necessary to go at this point. The fact remains that to go directly to biology or physics in the name of science is to give way to something that is in effect a superstition – the belief that a theory which is not cashable in physical or biological terms is, by that very fact, not worth having. In fact, folk psychology itself provides, at any rate at a certain level, a quite adequate understanding of human beings and of some animals (and I make the qualification over animals only because the great differences between higher and lower animals make generalizations about them extremely hazardous). Moreover, contrary to what is often said, our everyday understanding of human beings makes predictions about their behaviour quite possible on some occasions and for some people.

The question is sometimes asked whether folk psychology is itself a theory. That question is not entirely unambiguous. If what is meant by the question is whether folk psychology provides a system of connected concepts in terms of which sense can be made of human beings and their behaviour, then of course folk psychology constitutes a theory. If, on the other hand, there is any suggestion in the question that the acceptability of folk psychology is in any way uncertain or hypothetical, that is quite a different matter. There is nothing uncertain about the fact that people, often enough, do things because they believe that so doing will produce results which they wish to attain, whether or not that is always the way in which to explain what they do. To suggest that folk psychology is of no use for explanatory and predictive purposes has an air of absurdity about it – which is not to say that everyone is as good as anyone else in putting the theory to use in providing explanations or predictions of other people's behaviour. To be quite clear about this, however, one needs to know exactly what folk psychology is, and to this matter I shall turn in brief. I shall return to the same issues repeatedly throughout the book.

Whatever others have meant in speaking of 'folk psychology' I at any rate mean our common-sense understanding of people, how they see things, their thoughts, their wants and their behaviour. The principles of such understanding are not to be found, or not necessarily to be found in any textbook of psychology or philosophy, although that does not rule out the possibility of psychologists and philosophers trading on that understanding. Folk psychology is not a theory constructed for scientific purposes, although, as I said earlier, that does not mean that it is not a theory in some sense of that term. There is a common-sense understanding of ordinary physical things also, a folk physics as one might put it. Science has deepened that understanding almost beyond all measure, and there is no reason why a scientific psychology should not deepen our understanding of people and their behaviour; if it is thought that there are limits on what has been achieved in that way so far, that may be due to, amongst other things, the complexity of the subject-matter. Physics has not produced any reasons for the abandonment of our common-sense understanding of ordinary things, or at all events it has not suggested the complete abandonment of that understanding, however much it has suggested its modification in important areas. If, perhaps *per impossibile* or at least *per improbabile*, it should suggest that we should give up totally all that we believe about the world and all that we presuppose in our everyday commerce with it, that suggestion would be received quite rightly with utter scepticism. Modification yes, but abandonment no. For analogous reasons any suggestion on behalf of so-called 'scientific psychology' that our common-sense understanding of people and their behaviour is unreliable and should be abandoned altogether should be received with similar total scepticism.

The question still remains in which direction from folk psychology a scientific psychology should go. I shall return to this question later in the book at various points. All that needs to be pointed out at this point is that it cannot be assumed without argument and without due regard to the facts that it should move in the direction of physics, physiology or even computational theory. The truth may be that with regard to the relation between psychology and these other disciplines we are as much in the dark as we ever were. To repeat, my aim in what follows is to take the conception that we should regard human beings and animals as a kind of box with input and output and to ask how that conception must be refined if it is to have any psychological reality.

1

Behaviourism

BEHAVIOUR, STIMULUS AND RESPONSE

I suggested in the Introduction that there is a sense, even if it is, historically, a somewhat misplaced one, in which behaviourism can be viewed as an attempt to understand and predict human and animal behaviour purely in terms of connections between input and output. The input consists of stimuli; the output consists of responses, and what comes in between is of no concern to the theory. That theory is often characterized in consequence as being an 'S–R' theory; stimulus and response are all that matters. This, however, is not all that there is to it, because the theory relies upon specific conceptions of stimulus and response. Charles Taylor[1] has suggested that this conception is a 'mechanistic transposition of the traditional empiricist views on epistemology'. The traditional empiricist epistemology in question is the one to be found in the British Empiricists and in Hume in particular. It involves an atomism, in Hume's case an atomism of impressions and ideas such that all complex impressions and ideas are derived from corresponding simple ones while all simple ideas are copies of corresponding impressions. As far as behaviourism is concerned the more immediate precedent is to be found in nineteenth-century sensationalism and associationism, theories which similarly embraced the thought that all the contents of the mind are derived from simple sensations and that the only principle governing possible connections between one idea and another is that of association. The atoms presupposed by behaviourism are basic stimuli and responses and the only principle governing possible new connections between stimulus and response is that of conditioning.

This was more or less explicitly asserted by J. B. Watson, the father of behaviourism,[2] who thought that all behaviour was analysable into complexes of learned and unlearned responses to stimuli. The acquired connections between stimulus and response that result from learning all come about by the process of conditioning, the conception of which was established, or ostensibly established, by Pavlov. I say 'ostensibly established' because, although Pavlov suggested that the salivary response in his dogs was made to occur in response to the sound of a bell, rather than as a natural response to the smell of food, because of an association between the two stimuli, there is much in the actual experimental situation that he used, which involves motivational considerations and casts doubt on the suggestion that the behaviour is due to mere association between stimuli. (I have in mind the fact that the dogs had to be made hungry and that they were prevented from running around in search of food.) I shall return to that issue later.

The point on which I wish to concentrate at the moment is the ambiguity of the terms 'stimulus' and 'response'. It is no news that this ambiguity exists; it has been pointed out by several commentators.[3] The most basic sense of 'stimulus' in a biological context must involve the idea of the application of some form of energy to a nerve ending. The form of energy so applied may differ from case to case; all that is important is that the nerve fires when the energy is applied. In the situation typified by Pavlov's experiments, however, the stimulus involves much more than this. In the case of the so-called unconditioned stimulus – that which naturally produces the salivary response – what brings about that response is a smell, something that on the face of it presupposes some form of perception on the part of the dogs. The so-called conditioned stimulus also seems to involve perception in that the dogs are responding to a heard sound. It might indeed be argued that they are taking the sound of a bell as a sign of food to come. But it might be premature to jump to that conclusion straight away, since a possible construal of the situation is that it is the stimulation of nerves in the nose and ear that produces the effect in the two cases. Why, however, should such stimulation produce such effects?

The answer to that question or ones like it is clearest where the response is a reflex. The notion of a reflex has generally been recognized as involving something of an abstraction, in the sense that although certain bodily reactions seem to occur quite naturally and instinctively in response to certain causes, for example, the contraction of the pupil of the eye in response to bright light, to think of that comprising a reflex is to think of its involving a specific connection between stimulus and reaction in abstraction from the rest of the nervous system. The notion of a reflex presupposes that of the reflex arc, the idea of an arc of neural connections starting from the nerve endings affected, proceeding to the central nervous system, and back to the muscle contracted (or whatever else it is that happens). That so-called reflexes can sometimes be inhibited is an indication of the fact that in supposing the existence of such a neural connection we are ignoring possible ramifications within the nervous system, which may make inhibition possible. Nevertheless, the idea of such a simple connection in a reflex arc is at least intelligible. Pavlov relied upon that idea in his theory of the conditioned response, since he supposed that conditioning takes place as a result of one stimulus being substituted for another in the context of such a neural connection. Conditioning is on that theory simply stimulus substitution. Whether or not anything of that kind literally takes place, it is at least intelligible that it should do so, and if it does, then, given the idea of an original reflex, the question why stimulation of this kind produces the effects that it does is answered.

Where, however, neither the idea of a reflex nor that of stimulus substitution has any application it is a different story; and it is not obvious even in the Pavlov situation that these notions do have genuine application. Dogs need to be hungry in order to salivate to the smell of food; the stimulation of the nerves of the nose does not, surely, produce salivation unless that condition is satisfied. Furthermore, salivation at the sound of a bell in these circumstances does not seem to be just a matter of so reacting to the stimulation of certain nerves of the ear. Some sensitivity to these issues on the part of psychologists is indicated by the fact that there eventually came to be made a distinction between classical conditioning as so far described and instrumental conditioning, in the case of which the animal or person responds in such a way that the response can be seen as a means to some end. A situation is most plausibly to be seen in this latter way when it is accepted also that the so-called stimulus is being taken as a sign of something, for example, when the sound of a buzzer is taken by the subject as a sign of a coming shock. The salivation of the dogs in Pavlov's experiment can be viewed up to a point in the same way. I have already indicated that the sound of the bell might in that situation be considered as treated by the dog as a sign of food to come; the only difficulty in classifying it in consequence as a case of instrumental, rather than classical, conditioning is that, unlike the removal of the hand from a contact to prevent the possibility of receiving a shock, salivation is not obviously a means to any end.

The situation is complicated still further when one brings in what Skinner has called operant conditioning.[4] When a rat presses a lever in a so-called 'Skinner box' in order to produce a food pellet to satisfy hunger, the behaviour is certainly instrumental, but, as is made clear by the invocation of the notion of an operant, rather than that of response, to indicate what is conditioned, this is not, strictly speaking, conditioning in either of the two senses so far set out. As I have tried to argue elsewhere in greater detail,[5] these shifts in the sense of 'conditioning', as applied to these different cases, cast doubt on its utility as a theoretical concept. There is even doubt whether conditioning according to the official Pavlovian paradigm ever occurs, and that doubt has been expressed even by psychologists in the behaviourist tradition.

I shall not here go further into that consideration; my concern, after all, is with the interpretations that those in that tradition put upon the notions of input and output. One further comment, however, is called for about the Skinnerian notion of an operant. On the face of it the sort of thing that Skinner is talking about under this heading, for example, the pressing of a lever by a rat, is most plausibly construed as an action on the animal's part. Of course, a response too might be regarded similarly as an action, but that is not what it is on the official paradigm, and it is that paradigm which establishes the sense of the term within the theoretical structure. Moreover, salivation is certainly not to be construed as an action on the dog's part; it is a straightforward bodily reaction. What seems to have gone on, therefore, in the thinking of those in the behaviourist tradition is a stretching of the concept of a reaction, through that of a response, to that of an operant, which is in effect that of an action. The stretching of a theoretical concept is not in general objectionable in science; it depends on whether the stretching involves useful analogies between the things to which the concept is then given application. It is arguable that in the present case the stretching has gone too far. That this is so can be seen from the following.

The situation is in fact similar to that which we earlier saw to hold good with respect to the notion of a stimulus. In that case the notion has been stretched from what is simply the application of a form of energy to a nerve ending, through anything that produces some form of response in an organism, to a feature of something in the environment which is perceived by the animal or person in a certain way. Analogously, on the response side, there has been a move from the idea of a reaction caused in a straightforward way by something in the animal's or person's environment, whether that environment be external or internal, through the idea of a response which may be, so to speak, activated by something in the environment (it is after all a *response*) but is not caused by it in a straightforward way, to the idea of an act or action, which may be made in relation to something in the environment but need not be activated by it in any significant sense.

Watson, indeed, thought of an act as simply a set or collection of responses or reactions. The atomism of which I spoke earlier is evident in this, in that it is supposed that it is possible to identify and distinguish such individual responses or reactions by themselves without this presenting anything in the way of a problem. Acts were, in Watson's view, no more than complex sets of such atomic responses. There is no difference of nature in what occurs, merely one of complexity. On the side of the stimulus, Watson said that a complex set of stimuli amounted to what he called a 'situation'. In ordinary parlance a situation is something that may be said to obtain in the world and can in principle be seen to obtain. It is certainly not a complex set of applications of energy to nerve endings. That is not to say that when someone perceives a situation there may not be a complex set of applications of energy to nerve endings. But perception is not just that, and what else has to obtain in order for it to be true that someone perceives a situation or perceives it in a certain way is a matter to which I shall return in due course. Likewise, an action is not just a set of reactions to the environment, not a set of muscle movements of the kind that one may expect in the case of a reflex. Once again, that is not to say that when one acts there may not be a complex set of muscle movements; indeed one would normally suppose that there is just that, although there may be acts of mind in which nothing of the kind occurs. But even when the act is bodily there is more to saying that the act is performed than saying that such and such muscle movements are taking place.

It may still be asked, however, what is wrong with saying that the input is to be analysed in terms of sets of atomic stimuli, given that I allow that the stimuli, in the form of the applications of energy to nerve endings, do actually exist, even when what one is doing is perceiving a situation. What is wrong equally with saying that the output is to be analysed in terms of muscle or other bodily movements? It should be noted, first, that I have not committed myself in what I have just said to any conception of *atomic* elements, whether on the input side or on the output side. It may seem obvious that it must be possible in principle to identify the stimulation of individual nerve endings and the movements of individual muscles, whether or not any of these can actually take place in isolation from the system to which each of them belongs. But that does not entail that the input at any given time is just the sum of individual stimulations, for what happens at one nerve ending may affect what happens at another. The same applies *mutatis mutandis* on the output side. But the idea of complexes of atomic elements brings with it the idea that those elements are independent of each other and indeed independent of anything else. The Watsonian conception of stimulus and response implies just that.

The main objection, however, to the idea that is mooted above is the same as the one that I noted in the Introduction to the suggestion that input and output might be construed in purely physical or biological (that is, physiological) terms – that it has nothing immediately to do with psychology. Watson in effect smuggles in what is psychologically relevant when he speaks of acts and situations, but he achieves his aim merely by a kind of subterfuge, in suggesting that acts and situations are no more than complex reactions and stimuli. Nor is this a local matter which applies only to Watson. For behaviourism in general inherited these ambiguities. As I said earlier, the ambiguities in the notion of 'stimulus' have often been noted. But the same applies to 'behaviour', the notion on which the whole movement is based. If psychology is the study of behaviour what exactly does it study? Not, surely, merely reactions to stimuli, nor merely complex sets of such reactions, however complicated. What behaviour is according to behaviourists remains therefore obscure.

The thought that behaviour is at any rate something which is bodily has appealed to those whose sympathies lie in the direction of physicalism; but that is a mistake also. To say that behaviour is bodily is to say that it takes a bodily form; it is not necessarily to say that all that occurs is bodily, or, in case that looks once again as if I am simply maintaining a position on the mind–body problem, it is not necessarily to say that what occurs can be analysed entirely into complexes of merely physical movements (movements, moreover, which simply occur, as opposed to being made by the behaver). Many philosophers have supposed, nevertheless that behaviourism is a form of physicalism, with the implication that all that occurs in its view is mere physical movements or other similar occurrences. It is conceivable that if most behaviourists had been asked what ontology they were committed to they would have answered in a way that implied a commitment to physicalism. But on the ordinary sense of 'behaviour' there is no such commitment. Moreover, even that behaviour which is bodily need not be analysable into complexes of physical occurrences, although the theoretical framework of behaviourism may suggest otherwise.

The confusion evident in all this has recently led, as if as a corollary, to a change of usage in the word 'behaviour' at any rate on the part of many American philosophers and psychologists. There has been an increasing tendency recently to use the word 'behaviour' in the plural. Once, when as editor of *Mind* I protested about this to someone, I was told that it was not a mere grammatical solecism, but a conceptual change. In a way, I think that that is true, but I do not believe it to be a change for the better. By 'behaviours' might be meant forms of behaviour, but I believe that the conceptual shift goes deeper than that, and that the issue is not a trivial one. The use of the plural suggests that 'behaviour' in the singular picks out a distinct identifiable item, and that the plural then picks out a collection of these. That is the very conception which is endemic in Watsonian behaviourism. I suggest that that particular way of thinking on the part of psy-

chologists has infected a whole way of thinking about behaviour
itself. Hence the kind of misconception about behaviour which I
have been anxious to point out is becoming incorporated into
common ways of talking – and, I think, thinking. This might well
be viewed as something of a disaster.

TELEOLOGY

One other objection that has been made to behaviourism is that it
fails to take account of the teleological processes which are
involved in the behaviour of men and animals. When Taylor says,
as I noted earlier, that behaviourism is 'a mechanical transposition of traditional empiricist views on epistemology' he is not only
drawing our attention to the atomism which is inherent in behaviourism in ways similar to what holds good of Humean epistemology and other philosophical theories which derive from that.
There is also the implicit criticism that behaviourist theory is
mechanist, when it should not be. Against mechanism is set
teleology. Unfortunately, there is a certain ambiguity in that term
which tends to blunt the force of the criticism. I have already
suggested, without so far elaborating the suggestion to any extent, that if an adequate psychological understanding of humans
and some animals is to be provided the output must be construed
as action. The concept of action presupposes that of intention,
and although much needs to be said about that, and something
will be said about it later in this book, it is reasonable to indicate
now that much if not all action may be described as purposive.
When engaged in purposive activity people have certain ends or
goals in view (something that in turn presupposes consciousness
of some kind). In that sense what happens when they so act can
rightly be said to be teleological.

  The term 'teleological' can, however, be applied to quite
different things – in particular to systems within which certain
components play certain roles or functions in maintaining the
function of the whole. In that case they contribute to the attainment or maintenance of something which is the end or goal of the
system. Indeed, there is normally a tendency of the system to
exhibit a pattern of behaviour which converges on to an end-
state, and when that is attained the system reverts to a stable state

until disturbed, when the pattern is set up again. That is how it is with servo-systems, such as thermostats or, with modifications about the end-state, to guided missiles. In such cases, it would normally be accepted that the goal-directed nature of the activity is such that what happens can be explained in mechanical terms also; but, as Taylor rightly asserts, there can be no *a priori* argument to the effect that this must be so in the case of all goal-directed systems. Whether it is so or not is a matter of empirical fact. It would be quite wrong, however, to say that such systems were purposive in the sense that some of the activity of human beings clearly is, as noted above. For one thing, there is absolutely no need that such systems be conscious of the end to be pursued. For another, it is far from obvious that when human beings act purposively the pattern of their activity is always goal-directed in the sense that we can see, at any rate in principle, their activities as converging on to a single goal, the attainment of which brings about the cession of the goal-directed activity.

For the last reason, as well as others, it would be wrong to try to construe purposive behaviour as goal-directed behaviour in which the agent is simply conscious of the goal. Spinoza once said that if a stone thrown through the air was conscious it would think that it was flying of its own volition (and Schopenhauer added, for reasons of his own, that the stone would be right!). What Spinoza says is difficult to assess if only for the reason that one cannot tell what delusions conscious beings may be subject to. Equally one cannot have any idea of what a conscious stone might think in these circumstances. Would *we* think that we were flying of our own volition if we were thrown through the air? Whatever we might think, we would certainly be quite wrong to think that we were flying of our own volition. *Ex hypothesi* we were doing nothing of the kind. Analogously, if a thermostat were conscious, it would be quite wrong for it or for us to think that the mainten- ance of the temperature of a room, secured by its means, was brought about by the fulfilment of its purpose.

Taylor, on the other hand, does seem to think that purposive behaviour can be construed as teleological activity plus conscious- ness. For, in the exposition of his views, he first sets out an account of teleological explanation, and then proceeds to an account of explanation in terms of purpose via a story about consciousness. Moreover, the main fault that he finds with behaviourism is that it seeks to establish laws governing behaviour which are of the wrong form. Behaviourists suppose that the laws in question, if they can be discovered, will be strictly causal in such a way that they can be backed up by a mechanistic theory. In fact, Taylor suggests, any laws that can be discovered in this area must be teleological in form.

There has been much argument among philosophers about the exact nature of teleological explanation and its form. Taylor suggests with some plausibility that the form of a teleological explanation is that, given a system and background conditions, that an event B is required or necessary for the attainment of a certain goal G is a sufficient condition of B's occurrence. Thus, for example, given a thermostat and certain conditions of environmental temperature, that the opening of the thermostat is required in order to raise the temperature level to a certain point is a sufficient condition of that very thing happening. Taylor speaks of such a system as purposive, but it is that only in the sense that it has been designed with certain purposes and its functioning is such as to subserve those purposes. It is far from clear that purposive behaviour, as it manifests itself in human beings, is always goal-directed in the sense that has been explained; it depends on the circumstances whether a human being acting with a purpose behaves in such a way that his behaviour is and can be seen as directed towards an identifiable goal.

Taylor suggests that because his account of the matter presupposes a system as background, and because the event to be explained is to be identified simply by reference to a goal to which it is directed and not independently, the account presupposes a form of holism which is inconsistent with mechanism. Hence the form of the laws involved in any teleological explanation is incompatible with mechanism, and the laws in question cannot be causal laws in the ordinary sense. When one turns to the form of explanation which is involved in the explanation of action of a purposive kind, Taylor grants that more is required than that the action 'result or meet the criterion by which actions of this kind are characterized'. It must also be the case 'that the agent's intention or purpose was to achieve this result or criterion' (p. 29).

Later (p. 33), he adds that the relation between intention and the behaviour which is performed because of it is not a contingent one, for it is part of what we mean by 'intending X' that 'in the absence of interfering factors, it is followed by doing X'. This has been put by other philosophers, for example, Norman Malcolm,[6] by saying that the principles involved in the explanation of action by reference to purpose are *a priori*. This can be so only if such principles are *ceteris paribus* principles (that is, principles which hold good only if other things are equal), as is suggested by Taylor's reference to the absence of interfering factors. It is indeed arguably the case that if someone intends to do X he will do it *other things being equal*, but then much turns on what makes things equal and unequal. However this may be, it has no bearing on the question of the form of teleological laws. Taylor may well be right about what he says the form of teleological laws is without being right about the nature and status of the principles which are appealed to in explaining action in terms of purpose. The two issues are quite separate, or at least seem to be so and ought to be assumed as so unless there is further argument to the contrary.

It follows from all this that the crucial objection to behaviourism cannot be that it is mistaken about the form of the laws which govern behaviour. Teleological laws are indeed different in form from causal laws which presume a background of mechanics. But if there are any laws governing behaviour they are not teleological in that sense; they involve reference to purpose at some point, and purpose, as we have seen, involves more than teleology plus consciousness. What is wrong with behaviourism is that it is mistaken, not about the *form* of the laws governing behaviour, but about their *content*.[7] It is mistaken, that is, about the nature of the concepts involved in our thinking about behaviour. Indeed, it is mistaken about the very concept of behaviour itself. It is perfectly true that we speak of the behaviour of all sorts of things, including straightforwardly physical things, and in so speaking we mean to speak of the pattern of movement which they exhibit. But when we speak of human (and indeed much animal) behaviour, we are not concerned simply with such patterns of movement; we are concerned with what people (and animals) *do*. Similarly, on the input side, we are concerned, in relation to what people do, not simply with what affects them in the way that a stimulus may do, but with how they perceive the world around them. All these concepts, together with many others, such as that of belief, in terms of which we sum up what holds good of a person cognitively, are missing from the behaviourist conceptual scheme, and it is for this reason that it cannot do justice to that very thing which it purports to deal with exclusively – behaviour.

What this means is that the defects of behaviourism do not lie simply in its deliberate failure to consider what goes on inside the organism, however 'inside' is to be interpreted in this context. Its main defects flow from an inadequate theoretical apparatus for dealing with what it should be dealing with. Nevertheless, our next step must be to consider what going inside the black box entails or should be taken to entail. That is the purpose of the next chapter.

2

Going Inside the Black Box

INFORMATION AND INFORMATION PROCESSING

It is entirely natural that one who is dissatisfied with behaviourism as an explanatory theory of human behaviour should contemplate providing the requisite explanation by adopting a centralist approach. That is to say that the next natural step to take is to go inside the black box and attempt to explain what happens at the periphery by reference to what goes on inside. If that were totally achievable, of course, the box would no longer be black, but to the extent that we are still ignorant of the intervening processes between input and output the box must remain of varying degrees of greyness and opaqueness. Hence, it is important that we should become clear about what sorts of intervening processes are relevant to the enterprise contemplated. Moreover, what sorts of intervening processes *could* be relevant must surely depend on how the input and output processes themselves are construed. If, for example, one had in mind by input merely the imposition of physical energy on the system, and by output merely the output of physical energy in some way by the system, it would be natural to explain the connection between the two simply by reference to those purely physical processes which intervene between input and output so construed. As I have said several times already, that would have nothing to do with psychology, and the human organism is so complicated in any case that the thought that one could gain much understanding of it in this way seems hopeless.

What, however, about an appeal to physiology? Since the human organism is a biological entity which functions, at any rate in large part, on physiological principles, an appeal to physiology seems a natural course of action. If all that we were concerned to do was to provide an explanatory theory which would set out and explain the connection between stimulus and consequent reaction, that would be fine. At this point, however, we see the ambiguities of interpretation which existed in the case of behaviourism arising yet again. For no construal of input and output that is psychologically relevant can be formulated simply in terms of stimulus and reaction. To emphasize that point is not to say that an appeal to physiology has no relevance to an understanding of how we behave as a result of our perception of the world, where that behaviour is more than mere reaction as at present conceived. Clearly a suitably adapted physiological apparatus is necessary for us to respond to the environment in this way. Moreover, there must be some relation between the nature and structure of that apparatus and how we see the world and how we behave in relation to it. In addition, defects in that apparatus, as with certain forms of brain damage, may typically produce specific defects in our way of seeing the world or in reacting appropriately to it. Nevertheless, to suppose that we can construe input and output themselves in purely physiological terms and explain the connection between them in similar physiological terms would be to contemplate the possibility of a theory which would be both overwhelming in its complexity if it were to have any pretensions to comprehensiveness and remote from anything psychological.

What I said just now about the relevance of physiological defects to this whole issue raises a question of some generality concerning the point of the investigation of defects and failures for a possible understanding of how people perceive the world and act appropriately to it. In the field of the psychology of perception the study of illusions is a well-established part of the subject and of approaches to it. An illusion is in effect a defect in our way of seeing the world, in that in its case we fail to see the world as it actually is. A discovery of the reasons for the failure, the causes of the illusion, can well cast light on the question how we manage to see the world correctly when we do so, and on the question what makes it possible for us so to do. Not all psychologists of perception have accepted this point of view. J. J. Gibson,[1] for example, puts a minimum of weight on the advantages which may accrue from a study of illusions; but that is, at least in part, because he wants to have nothing to do with the question of what in us makes it possible for us to see the world as it is and because he thinks it sufficient to point to the amount of information that is available in the so-called stimulus array. I shall return to this point in a later chapter. If, however, we accept that there must be features in us which make correct perception possible, it is clear enough that a study of illusions and their causes will help to identify those features. That is a point which has a quite general application to the conditions of any kind of performance. We need to know what are the conditions which make success in it possible. Hence, the study of the kinds of effect that are produced by certain brain defects may regularly be expected to cast light on how the skills involved in normal performance are organized and related both to each other and to the ends to which they are directed.

The other point which I mentioned in this connection – that there must be some relation between the nature and structure of the physiological apparatus and how we see the world and how we behave in relation to it – is less clear cut. The Gestaltists laid great emphasis upon a version of such a principle in their thesis of isomorphism: that there must be a similarity of structure between the so-called phenomenal field and the brain states which mediate it. That thesis led Wolfgang Köhler to postulate that brain states must be structured in a non-atomistic way, that is, so that the processes involved are holistic and not reducible simply to combinations of what goes on in individual nerves and synapses.[2] That theory met with no kind of general acceptance – reasonably so given what is known about the nature of the brain. That, however, does not end possible speculation about the ways in which the brain functions, given that general understanding of what it consists of. That it works on computational principles is now a widely accepted supposition, although exactly what principles is a matter of dispute. Nevertheless, alternative hypotheses have been put forward from time to time, such as the suggestion by Karl Pribram that it works on holographic principles or the recent suggestion that it works on the basis of 'parallel distributed processing'.[3] The plausibility of any such model of the working of the brain depends essentially upon how far it fits the psychological phenomena which it purports to explain. That is a very obvious point, but it nevertheless requires emphasis. Moreover, the fitting in question must be one which holds good in detail. As the history of the thesis of isomorphism indicates, a *general* similarity between certain characteristics of brain structure and the psychological phenomena to be explained by its means is not enough.

What seems to follow from all this is that if one attempts to explain the behaviour of people in relation to how they see the world by going direct to physiology one will at best be laying out some of the conditions the satisfaction of which makes behaviour of this kind in these circumstances possible. If, on the other hand, one has no commitment to the notions of behaviour and perception as they are properly to be understood (and this entails having some concern for folk psychology), but construes the input and output directly in physiological terms, the project will be too distant from anything that is psychologically relevant. For one will be considering the phenomena at the level of the stimulation of nerve-endings, the consequent neural excitation, and final efferent nerve action, so that what emerges at the end will be muscle contractions, glandular secretion and the like. Apart from the fact that this is still very far from having anything explicit to do with human perception, motivation and behaviour, the complexity of what is involved, and will have to be faced if it is to be brought into any relation with those psychological processes and facts, is almost as mind-boggling as the suggestion that the whole thing can be set out in terms of physics and physical energy. As I have tried to make clear above, physiology is far from being irrelevant to a consideration of psychological processes, but the link between the two is not direct. The psychological processes themselves have to be construed in terms which make the relation between them and the mechanisms that mediate them and make them possible intelligible.

One way of conceivably achieving that aim, at any rate as far as the input side is concerned, is to think of the input to the organism in information-processing terms. For it seems natural to think that the processes of perception involve the receipt of information about the environment, and that that information has to be processed in some way if it is to be of use to the organism in connection with what it has to do. Indeed, put in those very general terms, the supposition in question is not only natural; it is undeniable. For whatever other function perception has, it must involve that of providing information about the environment; moreover, whatever information is available in that way has to be made explicit and made sense of, so that the need to process that information seems inevitable. That sense of 'information', however, is a quite ordinary one and in itself has no implications for the kinds of mechanisms which are needed to make the processing possible. Moreover, it is, to use the language of J. J. Gibson in this respect,[4] 'information about', and to think of matters in these terms is in effect to embrace what has become known as intentionality, at least in the sense that whatever processes take place are directed to something else as their object. (What else there is to the notion of intentionality, which has become something of a cult-notion for those working in this area, will appear later.[5]) How intentionality in this sense is possible is one of the largest issues in this area, and the question is not bypassed simply by an appeal to the notion of information.

Because of this, recourse has sometimes been had to a different and technical sense of 'information', that derived from so-called information theory. Indeed Fred Dretske's *Knowledge and the Flow of Information*[6] is an attempt to base a whole theory of knowledge and of its acquisition on such information theory. The problem with the project lies in the nature and origin of information theory itself. It arose out of a consideration of information transmission systems, such as telegraphy. Because of the deficiencies which may exist in a telegraph or telephone cable the electric impulses which are set up at one end of it are not likely to be exactly the same as those which reach the other end as a result of the transmission process. Because of this, the receiver needs to be provided with some estimation of the probability that the impulses received do constitute a real message and are not simply due to chance. The more probable it is that the patterning of impulses received is not mere 'noise', is not due to chance, the more probable it is that a genuine message is being transmitted and that its nature is as received.

It follows that the actual amount of information received by a transmission system of this kind is a function of the improbability of the patterning of impulses being due to chance. Equally, once given a reliable system for the transmission of information in this way, the amount of information to be derived from a given situation is a function of the number of ways in which that situation can be construed if those ways are equi-probable. If there are no alternative ways in which the situation can be construed then the degree of probability that the one way of construing it is right by chance is at a minimum, and the amount of information derived is at a maximum. Since a plausible view of knowledge is that for X to know p, X's belief that p must be such that it is no accident, not a chance matter, that it is the truth that is believed, there is an obvious connection between the thought that X has maximum information in this sense about a situation and the thought that X has knowledge about it.

It is on a thought of this kind that Dretske in effect relies in his attempt to set out a theory of knowledge and its acquisition in terms of information theory. But, as should be evident from my account, the context in which information theory gets application is one in which it is taken as read that one person is attempting to communicate with another. Otherwise the question whether a certain patterning of impulses in a cable is or is not due to chance would have no importance; and the same applies to the question about the number of ways in which a situation can be construed. Hence, the theory presupposes a context of ordinary human communication and what that presupposes in turn about what is requisite in a human being if he is to be either a communicator or a receiver of information. It is not surprising, therefore, that it is possible to set out a theory of knowledge and of its acquisition in information-theory terms; for that theory itself presupposes the sort of thing which in that case it is being used to explain. Communication implies knowledge on the part of the communicators. Much of the theory as used by Dretske in this way involves in consequence a translation into technical terms of our ordinary, folk-psychological, accounts of knowledge, its communication and transmission, and its acquisition. One cannot, therefore, expect from information theory an account of the kinds of perceptual relations in which we stand to the world which will get round the back of our ordinary, common-sense, understanding of what perception is. If we are to analyse that understanding in information-processing terms in such a way that it provides a genuine alternative to folk psychology it is impossible to do that via information theory alone.

In saying this I have not in any way done justice to the complexities of Dretske's account. He recognizes, for example, that what he calls a 'semantic theory of information' (one that brings in the idea of 'meaning') is more than 'information theory' at its basic level. But he suggests that the semantic character of information – its intentionality so to speak – derives from the intensional character of the natural laws in virtue of which what occurs at one end of a communication system is nomically dependent on what happens at the other (pp. 75ff., 81). To say this is to reflect the idea, inherent in what is known as the 'causal theory of knowledge', that the non-accidental connection between the knower and the facts is due to the fact that the knowledge process involves a reliable causal connection. It is also suggested, as has been maintained by others but remains entirely controversial, that intentionality is simply a matter of the non-extensional character of the laws expressing that connection. (Indeed, that suggestion even affects the spelling of 'intentional/intensional'; Dretske actually speaks of the *intentional* character of the causal laws in question.)

Dretske has gone on subsequently[7] to stress that if a system is to be such that it can operate on the basis of information as a knower does, it must be possible for it to get things wrong, as well as getting things right, and he has offered an account of how that is possible. Many recent writers in this area have expressed the hope that systems of the kind which we are concerned with (systems which, for reasons which will appear later, are termed representational systems) can take in the requisite connection with truth/falsity or rightness/wrongness via their functioning on teleological principles (that is, as involving teleology in the sense of that term which does not involve purpose but something more like function).[8] It is thereby supposed that an appeal to a naturalized form of teleology will do the trick by bringing in the ideas of something fulfilling or failing to fulfil a function. In his paper 'Misrepresentation' Dretske suggests that more is required than that alone. He supposes, however, that, given such a functional context, misrepresentation can be shown to be possible if one brings in something like conditioning or associative learning. For in that case, while the function of the system is to respond in a certain way when some feature holds good of the environment, it may in fact respond to something which is indirectly connected with that, as a result of conditioning or associative learning. The indirectness of the connection between it and that something may give rise to a breakdown in that connection, so admitting the possibility of error.

To speak of error on this account of the issues, however, is merely to say that as a matter of contingent fact the system does not respond to what it should do from the point of view of its function. It is far from clear that this is enough to allow us to speak of its getting things wrong, as is required if we want to speak equally of a breakdown of knowledge. The whole account raises large questions about whether learning in a sense adequate for the purpose is sufficiently explicated in terms of such ideas as that of conditioning or associative learning as Dretske conceives that.[9] If one brought in the notion of purpose and ideas of learning connected with that, it might be another matter. But that would spoil the point of the exercise which begins with *Knowledge and the Flow of Information* – to break down conceptions of knowledge, purpose and other such notions to conceptions of processes which take a naturalized and certainly non-normative form, even if they depend for their reliability on their conformity to nomically causal laws.

Although I do not think that this goal can be achieved, my immediate purpose has been to argue that one cannot rely for an understanding of what is involved in the ideas of perception and the acquisition of knowledge simply on the notion of information as employed in information theory. That notion presupposes, though indirectly, the ordinary notions of information which, ostensibly, it was supposed to explain. To say, as Dretske in effect does in *Knowledge and the Flow of Information*, that we should not worry very much about the use of the term 'information' in information theory (it can be spelled out in terms of the idea of conditional probabilities), but simply use it to build up our ordinary ideas of information, knowledge, etc. is to embark upon a programme of naturalized epistemology, the problems in which become evident in Dretske's later thought, as I have tried to indicate. Epistemologically, as I have said, the programme is on a par with attempts to explain knowledge in terms of the idea of attaining truth as a result of reliable causal connections between the knower and the facts, with error being due to the breakdown of such connections. While I think that the existence of such connections is sometimes what eliminates the possibility that it is an accident that it is the truth that is attained, for example, the knowledge of the place of a limb may depend on no more than the reliable causal processes involved in the workings of the sensory part of our nervous system, I do not think that this is always the case. As will appear later, I think that the concept of knowledge has in any case an essentially normative aspect[10] which makes it impossible, even with an appeal to teleology, to produce an entirely naturalized account of the process of attaining knowledge and of getting things wrong. I shall return to the concept of knowledge and to the conditions for its application in a later chapter.

COMPUTATION AND COGNITIVE SCIENCE

An alternative way, or perhaps, since Dretske invokes this also, an additional way, of thinking of the receipt and use of information which is not, on the face of it, the ordinary common-sense one is that which is involved in our understanding of the computational processing of information. It is after all normal to think of information being fed into a computer; then computational processes are carried out, as a result of which the information is processed, with an eventual output. For this to be possible the so-called information which is fed into the computer has to be put in a coded form which the computer can 'read' in whatever way it is programmed to do so. The information in question is thus in those codes, which are 'significant' to the computer only if it is programmed to interpret the codes accordingly. Most conceptions of information processing as applied to an understanding of human beings rely on this model.

It has to be noted, however, that what is fed into the computer can function as information only if the computer is designed and subsequently programmed to treat it in that way. That is why what is fed in can be regarded as a code – because a code is subject to certain principles of construction and interpretation, and in the case under consideration such principles are involved in the design and programming of the computer. The utility of all this depends on the wants and purposes of the designer and user of the computer, and this affects also whether what is fed into the computer constitutes information in any genuine sense. If we think of the human nervous system as functioning in a computational way, it is important to recognize too that what is fed into that system will have significance for the organism only in relation to what the organism has to do in dealing with the environment.

It may seem natural to think of the pattern of excitation of a sense-organ, such as the retina of the eye, as the data-base on which the brain, working on computational principles, relies in its functioning. I once participated in a symposium along with two psychologists in which we were asked whether it was not correct to think of the pattern of excitation on the retina as the data-base for the computational operations of the brain in this way. The two psychologists said 'Yes' and I said 'No'. Fortunately for me, the chairman called the discussion to a close before we were able to try to answer the obvious next question, 'Why?'. My reasons for saying 'No' will, however, become clearer later when I go into detail concerning the nature and preconditions of perception. But something can be said now on this matter. The most important point is the one that I have already mentioned – that the significance of the information provided in that pattern of excitation on the retina is not merely a matter of how it relates to the nature and programming of the nervous system (if this is thought of in computational terms), but of how it relates to what the organism as a whole has to *do* in dealing with the environment.

One reason why it is tempting to think in the terms which I am criticizing is that it may well be thought that, in folk-psychological terms, the information provided is, at least in part, a matter of what beliefs that organism acquires by its means. Indeed, it might be suggested that it is only in terms of that thought that it is plausible to regard the data-base as constituting information. Otherwise what is fed in is merely certain structures which can be organized by the computer according to the principles which are entailed by its design and programming. Even to think of the input as constituting a code is to think of it as having a sense which is relevant to the formation of beliefs. But in the normal computer case the beliefs in question are those of the user; and they depend on what he is using the computer for. The computer's receiving information in the sense with which we are at present concerned does not in itself amount to the acquisition of beliefs, except in the sense that the user may acquire beliefs, through his use of what the computer makes possible. Much more is required for belief in something to be possible than mere receipt of information in the present sense.

To believe something is to believe it as true. Not all beliefs are, of course, true. Nevertheless, what one believes is either true or false, and to believe it is to believe it *as* true. But if someone is to be capable of that he must be capable of having certain attitudes to the world and to truth. Someone who had no concern whatever for truth and falsity could scarcely be said to believe anything. For truth and falsity are not any old properties of propositions, and to believe something as true is to accept it as having a certain status which matters in connection with our relations to the world in which we find ourselves. It has been said that belief is the attitude appropriate to the truth,[11] and there is much to be said for such a claim. But for present purposes the important point is that it is necessary to speak of *attitudes* in this connection.

The receipt of information is not in itself the acquisition of a belief; it is possible that the information might be too much to take, too much to accept. But if what is provided in this way had no relevance for belief it would not even be right to speak of information. One for whom truth and falsity had no importance whatever would not be in a position to have beliefs, and *a fortiori* what was provided for him would not be information. It follows that if the having of attitudes (which imply feeling of some kind) is necessary to the having and acquisition of beliefs, something that lacks that possibility could not have beliefs and could not be said to be in the position to receive information in any straightforward sense. A purely cognitive being would on that account be impossible, and the reference to such beings that sometimes occurs in science-fiction contexts is a reference to a myth.

I shall have more to say on that point later, but for present purposes the important thing to recognize is that to the extent that an information processor is construed in purely computational terms it *is* being construed as in effect a purely cognitive being. How could it, in that case, have any real concern with information proper? None of this is to say that it cannot be the case that part of our nervous system operates on computational principles. For just as computer operators may use what is provided by the operations of a computer to arrive at information and to process that information with reference to certain aims or goals, so one part of the system of which we are made up may have as its function the provision of something that may be used by other parts of the system in a way that is contributory to beliefs about the world in which we find ourselves. But it could not do this unless we were the sort of creature which could have beliefs in the first place, whatever may be the kind of mechanism which makes that possible in us.

There is a way in which what I have been saying about the sense of 'information' which is involved in information processing on computational principles connects up with what I said earlier about information theory and its use. As will be clear, both contexts presuppose a background story about beliefs and the aims and purposes of those who are using the information-processing systems in question. I said over information theory that Dretske's use of it involves a transformation into technical terms of our ordinary folk-psychological understanding of knowledge, its acquisition and transmission to others. This is so because we are given maximum information about what is put into one end of a communication transmission system when the pattern received is such that it is minimally probable that it is due to chance. This will be so when there is a law-like relation between what is received and what is put into the system. We rely on similar law-like connections when we take something observed as providing information about something. In that sense we can say that the number of rings in the sectioning of a trunk of a tree provides information about the tree's age. It does that because we know that a ring is the product of a year's growth and that there is a law-like connection between the number of rings and the number of years of growth. Hence there is a minimum probability that the number of rings in question is due to chance.

In other cases there may be other reasons why we may be justified in believing that something or other is a reliable sign of something else, so that the information which we receive concerning that other thing is thereby determined. In the case of information processing on computational principles we rely on the reliability of the coding principles. A system of coding is in effect a system of rules for the transformation of one thing into another. It is the reliability of those rules in a given system which determines the amount of information that is transmitted by its means. But it would transmit no information at all if human beings were not enabled to arrive at certain beliefs by its means. Analogously the law-like connection between the number of rings in the trunk of a tree and the number of years of its growth may or may not be an interesting fact, but it provides information about the number of years of growth only for those who can rely on the connection to arrive at beliefs and have an interest in doing so.

I have so far considered a number of possibilities for the construal of input into our 'black box', so that it provides the basis for a theory about the behaviour of human beings in relation to the world in which they find themselves. Physics and physiology proved both mind-boggling in their complexity as accounts of how input and output are to be mediated, and also too indirectly connected to anything that is psychologically relevant. The idea of information processing, whether construed in terms of so-called information theory or construed in computational terms, turned out not to be independent of the folk psychology which it was meant to replace; or at all events this is so if it is suggested that it might do the whole job, since nothing prevents the possibility of part of the mechanism which makes folk-psychological processes possible working on computational principles. Hence none of these theories can do justice to folk psychology without presupposing its truth or at all events its intelligibility. They are not both independent of and substitutions for it.

There are some commentators who brandish the label 'scientific psychology' in relation to any theory which depends essentially on physiology, and thereby disparage as unscientific any theory which relies on notions falling outside the physical/physiological domain. Apart from the fact that this involves the usurpation of the term 'scientific' in order to reserve it for the physical and biological sciences, it is no good insisting on the sanctity of scientific psychology so construed if it does not constitute an adequate *psychological* theory, or if it produces a theory so formidable in its complexity that it cannot make possible the predictions and explanations which we normally demand of a scientific theory. But exactly that is the case with a theory concerned with human beings if the input is construed in physical or physiological terms. In order to do justice to human behaviour as we ordinarily construe that, and in order to do justice to the thought that that behaviour is performed in relation to the world, information about which is provided by the senses, any adequate account of what intervenes and makes such behaviour possible will have to be fiendishly complex, so offending against canons of simplicity in scientific theorizing.

There is indeed a principle worth noting in this connection. This is that if the input to a system such as human beings comprise is to be considered as providing information which can then be acted on, then the weaker or thinner the construal of that input the more complex must be the construal of the inner and mediating states. This principle has in fact special implications for an understanding of learning; that is to say that it has special implications for an understanding of those inner processes which make possible *new* connections between input and output as a function of experience. Theorists such as Jerry Fodor who give large emphasis to internal states constituting mental representations, but give much less attention to the input processes which, supposedly, lead to the setting up of such internal states, have to suppose that all that makes new knowledge possible is there from the start; that is to say that it is innate.

There is much in this which is inherited from Chomsky, who has likewise claimed in relation to language-learning (and by implication to some other forms of learning to which the same principles apply) that one can understand that possibility only by assuming that we are born with certain innate structures or capacities, which are then put to use in relation to the world as hypotheses for which confirmation is sought in experience. But the supposition that that is how human beings proceed – by, simply, putting questions to nature as a scientist may be supposed to do – pays too little attention to the perceptual processes through which contact with the world is made in the course of experience. The same applies if we take the story about hypothesis construction simply as a metaphor and suppose, as Chomsky has done, that there exists a language-acquisition device which interacts with the environment. Because, as Chomsky has insisted, the data presented to such a device by language-speakers in the child's environment are 'corrupt', we have to suppose, it is claimed, that part of what is necessary for acquiring an understanding of language is embedded in the organism. Whatever else is to be said about these views, they seem to pay little regard to the complexities of *perception*, assuming some simple, perhaps causal, connection between things in the world and ourselves. It is thus no surprise, given the principle which I outlined above, that so much has to be built into the system itself in order to make good the shortcomings of the account of input to it. A thin account of the input entails for adequacy an excessively rich account of the inner states, and when learning enters the picture everything that matters has to be assumed as present in the system, if the acquisition of intelligible responses to such a thinly construed input is to be understood.

Some of the implications of the principle which I have set out can be seen too in some of Fodor's more recent writings, particularly his *The Modularity of Mind*.[12] In this book, Fodor sets out a three-level theory for cognitive psychology. There are central processes, working on the principles of scientific hypothesis confirmation, which are global, or as Fodor puts it Quinean, and isotropic in operation. That is to say that they work as a whole and cannot be divided into atomic elements, and (as far as isotropy is concerned) they are such that anything from any domain may be relevant to what is being considered. These processes are in consequence slow in comparison with what happens at the next lower level. They are also difficult, if not impossible to understand. Indeed Fodor jokingly (perhaps) refers to 'Fodor's First Law of the Nonexistence of Cognitive Science', which states that the more global a cognitive process is the less anybody understands it, and that very global processes are not understood at all, 'nor is there much hope that they ever will be' (p. 107). Secondly, there are input systems which are domain specific or modular and informationally encapsulated; they are also fast and have other properties by comparison with central processes which are responsible for the fixation of belief. The role of the input systems is to take what is handed on to them by the third, bottom, level processes, the sensory transducers, which detect forms of physical energy and transform them into a coded form such that the input systems can operate on them in an information-processing way.[13]

In all this, input is construed in terms of the transduction of physical energy into a coded, information-bearing, form so that it comprises data for computational processes. The domain specificity and informationally encapsulated character of the workings of the input systems mean that here too the processes contemplated are *from a cognitive point of view* simple or, as I put it earlier, thin, however complex they are simply as processes. From the point of view of what Fodor calls the fixation of belief, and indeed of all cognitive processes in their relation both to the environment and to possible action on the part of the organism in relation to the environment, the central processes are all-important, or at least supreme. But these are the processes which, on Fodor's account, we have the least chance of understanding because of their 'global' character. It follows that within the total theory the 'thin-ness' of the account of the input demands what now seems an unbearably rich account of the central processes – 'unbearably' because, given what is taken as understandable within the terms of reference of the theory, these processes now become outside the range of understanding. The fact that, in Fodor's view, much of the structure of input systems themselves is also innately determined does not affect that point.

In fact, of course, from the point of view of folk psychology we understand all these processes quite well, though not in the information-processing terms of transducers, input systems, coding and computational processes which constitute the Fodorean criteria of acceptability from a theoretical point of view. I say this here, although as will become apparent in the next chapter Fodor is, by comparison with a number of other people in this area, wedded to folk psychology. It may be important to note that Fodor's 'First Law', mentioned earlier, is a law of *cognitive science*; it is not a law of psychology in a more general sense. But if we construe the central processes in folk-psychological terms, that is, in terms of beliefs, wants and whatever other items we appeal to in explaining the behaviour of people, there is an inevitable problem of relating this to input if that is construed in information-processing terms.

In fact we have here a sophisticated version of the body–mind problem. If we construe the input in information-processing terms, we are invoking a theory the application of which to bodily processes at least makes sense, since we have some idea of what sort of hardware would fit the software implied by the computational processes invoked; whether that sort of hardware is realizable in the bodily processes which we believe to obtain is at least an intelligible question. We have little or no idea, however, what sort of hardware is appropriate for beliefs and other mental states of that kind. Hence, there is an inevitable gap between the central states on the folk-psychological interpretation and the input processes, if these are construed in the terms so far contemplated. That gap could be closed only by providing an adequate account of the central processes in computational or analogous terms, or alternatively by providing a different but adequate account of the input processes.

If Fodor is right in what he says about his 'First Law of the Nonexistence of Cognitive Science', the first of these alternatives is impossible. In that case, the only hope lies in the second alternative. More tough-minded theorists may wish to enter a sceptical reservation, to say the least, about Fodor's 'First Law'. But in that case it is important also to remember what in the end we are attempting to explain in whatever theory we are bringing to bear – behaviour. However we construe the input and the intervening processes, we have to bear in mind the nature of the output too. For, as I have tried to make clear earlier, it is the ambiguity in the interpretation of that, inherited from behaviourism, which is responsible for much of the inadequacy of the theories put forward in this area. So-called cognitive science does not stand by itself; even if its primary concern is the range of cognitive capacities possessed by human beings and some animals,[14] reference to such capacities would be empty if it did not help to explain the behaviour of those individuals in relevant situations.

Hence, to get a proper view of what is required we need to take account of the whole complex of input, intervening processes and output. It is no good confining one's attention simply to some part of this. If it is claimed that we do not need to note what is implied in the notion of behaviour, as we ordinarily understand that, an alternative construal of output must be forthcoming. Any alternative expressed in terms appropriate to physics or physiology alone gives rise to all the objections on the score of overwhelming complexity noted earlier, apart from the fact that such an account would have no connection with folk psychology and everything that would make the account psychologically relevant.

It becomes clear, once again, that proper accounts of input and output, so as to provide that psychological relevance, are what is required. Before turning to that, however, it is necessary to consider further the inside of our black box.

3

Inside the Black Box

INTENTIONALITY AND FUNCTIONALISM

If, as I said at the end of the last chapter, we construe the input and output processes to our black box in physical, physiological or information-processing terms, it will be necessary to construe the central, intervening processes in analogous terms. Moreover, there is a hierarchical arrangement to such processes; the putative physiological processes must be realizable in physical terms, and the putative computational or other information-carrying processes must be realizable in physiological terms. Otherwise there will be a lack of reality in the theory involved. It might, of course, be maintained that we do not need to have any concern for the reality of the theory, on the ground that such theories are instrumentalist anyway. That is to say that the only role of a scientific theory is to make adequate predictions possible, and that we do not need, for such purposes, to suppose that the terms of the theory actually refer to real things or processes. The dispute between realists and instrumentalists in the philosophy of science is an old one, dating from at least since the time of Pierre Duhem,[1] who was a committed instrumentalist in respect of physical theory. Whatever may be thought plausible in this respect in relation to physical theory, instrumentalism in psychology has a high degree of implausibility, if only for the reason that we are directly aware of certain states of mind in ourselves.

Instrumentalism in relation to psychology has been advocated nevertheless, particularly by Daniel Dennett.[2] He maintains that different attitudes on our part are demanded towards different kinds of system. But the systems themselves can be differentiated in fact only in terms of the stance that is called for on our part if we are to fare best in relation to them in respect of prediction and control. To certain systems, for example, the best stance in this respect is the 'design stance'; that is when the most adequate predictions can be made on the basis that the system is designed to further certain ends. The most important stance for present purposes is the 'intentional stance' which serves to differentiate 'intentional systems'. When we adopt that stance we speak of the system in terms of beliefs and the like. These are states which, as noted in chapter 2, involve intentionality, and do so in a sense derived somewhat loosely from the use of the term by the nineteenth-century Austrian philosopher Franz Brentano. He claimed that the mind was to be defined in terms of certain mental acts, all of which were related to objects which had *inesse* in respect of those acts. That is to say that the objects are, in a sense, simply internal to those acts. The objects to which the mind is directed in this way (by an *intentio animi*) need not exist in reality. Yet it would not make sense to think of the acts in question except in relation to an object of some kind, and it is for this reason that Brentano said that these objects have *inesse*; they exist only in relation to the act in question, and the relation between the act and the object is not a real relation. Belief, for example, can be false and for that reason does not necessarily stand in relation to any real state of affairs.

Intentionality looms large in discussions of the nature of states such as belief. For Dennett, however, a system is intentional only if an intentional stance is appropriate to it, and the stance will be appropriate only if, as a result, we can make adequate predictions in relation to the system. Whatever be the set-up of the system, we need not, on this basis, suppose that there actually exist in it any states properly to be called beliefs; it is purely a matter whether it is useful to think in this way. This is in spite of the fact that we might plausibly suppose that we are aware of the existence of beliefs in ourselves, and that in reporting and expressing our beliefs we do not suppose that we are merely adopting an intentional stance towards ourselves in the sense specified. But this last point is surely crucial. In other branches of science, such as physics, it might be an arguable matter whether in invoking a given theoretical concept there need be anything real answering it; one can at least give sense to the idea that the invocation of a certain theoretical notion might be useful for predictive purposes whether or not something answers to it in fact. That is scarcely plausible in the case of beliefs. That it may be predictively useful to think in terms of human beings as believers is neither here nor there; the fact is that we all know that we have beliefs. What these are is another matter, as is such questions as how beliefs are individuated, whether it is possible to have just one belief or whether any one belief presupposes a network of other beliefs, and so on. But that we do in fact have beliefs seems unarguable.

Fodor has, in an interesting and amusing article,[3] set out what is in effect a flow-chart of possible views in this area, such that certain considerations entail a choice between rival theories at various points along the way. As his chart makes clear, a rejection of instrumentalism does not necessarily entail the acceptance of beliefs as we ordinarily understand them. For someone may accept the necessity of appealing to beliefs as actual states, but deny that they are mental states as these are ordinarily understood. There are various ways in which this may be done, all of which entail some thesis about the real nature of beliefs which makes them other than we ordinarily suppose them to be. What is by ordinary standards the most implausible version of this is some form of eliminative materialism. In general terms this is a thesis to the effect that we can deal with the mind–body problem by asserting that mental states can be reduced in some way to physical states, and that when we come to accept this as true we shall eliminate references to mental states as such in our thought and talk.

One of the earliest versions of this thesis was put forward by Brian Farrell, but it has also been maintained by Richard Rorty, and has recently been espoused in a systematic and comprehensive way by Paul and Patricia Churchland.[4] To maintain any such view in a thoroughgoing way is to be exceptionally tough-minded, given that the view seems to fly in the face of common sense. In any case, unless one is inclined thereby to desert intentional concepts altogether and to be content with the purely extensional concepts of physiology, despite the overwhelming complexity of the resulting theory and its irrelevance to behaviour as such, one will have to take account of and offer an account of the nature of intentional states, such as belief, in order that one may know what such concepts can be reduced to. In other words one will have to know just what physiological states correspond to beliefs, wants, etc., and if there are problems over the individuation of beliefs these problems will carry over to the physiological states to which the beliefs are, supposedly, to be reduced.

A less radical thesis, and what many have considered to be a less objectionable thesis, is that it is in fact possible to produce an analysis of intentional states such as belief which will allow them to be realizable unproblematically in physiological terms. If such a thesis were sustainable it would give substance to the hope that, whether or not an account in physiological terms of what takes place when someone has a belief can be provided now, there is no logical or conceptual objection to that possibility. The chief form that such a thesis characteristically takes is to be termed functionalism. This theory in its general form constitutes a chapter in the story of the various vicissitudes of that form of physicalism which is known as token identity theory. According to that theory every token or individual mental state is to be taken as identical with some token or individual physical state, whether or not every type of mental state is identical with a given type of physical state. This is not the place to go into all the details of the functionalist form of that theory.[5] In any case, there is more than one variety even of that form. Moreover, it is at least possible to hold a version of functionalism according to which it is maintained, not that beliefs actually are states of mind the nature of which is to be explained in functional terms, that is, in terms of the role which they play in the general economy of the mind, but that we can explain human behaviour in terms of functional states of this kind, whether or not they correspond to beliefs.[6]

It is clear, with respect to this last version of the thesis of functionalism, that *if* a human being can be regarded, at all events in some respects, as a system within which certain components or sub-systems play roles within the general economy so as to link input and output, then those components or sub-systems *can* be identified in terms of the function which they perform. Indeed, one might think that it is one of the purposes of cognitive science to spell things out in this way. The only question, and it must by now be a familiar one, is how, without reference to anything else, one can specify the components or sub-systems in question. If the input and output were specifiable in physiological terms, one might conceivably suggest, *as a matter of hypothesis*, that there must be such and such internal components or sub-systems functioning in such and such a way, if there is a certain output when there is such and such input. But why should the functional entities or sub-systems hypothesized in this way have anything to do with what we might expect to be there on a psychological basis? They might indeed be quite different, and without the benefit of our knowledge of ordinary human psychology there would be nothing to provide guidance over what is to be hypothesized. Such a theory must either cheat by oblique reference to psychological concepts or be psychologically empty. Indeed that is, arguably, too charitable a view of the situation. One might bring a general knowledge of physiology to bear on the question what sorts of sub-system might conceivably link input and output, if these are themselves construed in physiological terms. But what is posited in this way might be positively misleading as an underpinning to psychology, unless one's knowledge of psychology told one what sort of thing to look for. Without that knowledge what is posited might be as little relevant to psychology as the details of a plumbing system.

It would be different if it was possible to sustain the thesis that what is to be understood by such things as beliefs is to be spelled out entirely in functional terms. If it were the case that to have a belief is simply to be in a state the whole nature of which is to fulfil a certain function within the mental economy, then it would be plausible that, however input and output are specified, one should look, in trying to link them, for, amongst other things, a system which functions in this way. For one would have the guidance in one's search provided by one's understanding of the nature of belief; and the same would be true of other mental concepts. It has indeed been the hope of many functionalists that just this would be the case, and that the functions in question might have a realization in physical or physiological terms. For in this way a form of physicalism or materialism might be sustained. Functionalism does not entail physicalism in itself, since the thesis that the whole nature of mental states might lie in their functional role does not in itself assert that that role is performed by physical items; as far as that goes the items might be mental. But functionalism leaves physicalism as a strong possibility.

But is it really the case that the whole nature of mental states lies in their functional role? Is all that we understand by the notion of belief something about the role performed by an item in an economy linking input and output? If not, it would be simply begging the question to suppose that an appeal to functionalism will do all that is required in providing a theory adequate for psychology. For that purpose, it would have to explain, additionally, why we do certain things when we perceive the world in a certain way. That would normally entail a story about the acquisition thereby of certain beliefs, in virtue of which, given a certain motivation, we act in such and such a way in relation to the world. There is now a very considerable literature on the adequacy of functionalism as a theory of the mind, including the question how functionalism can deal with sensations and the qualitative aspects of experience – what has come to be called *qualia*. I am not here concerned with the claim of functionalism to provide a general theory of the mind, although many have thought that *qualia* provide a severe and possibly insuperable obstacle to that project.[7] The question at present at issue is whether functionalism provides an adequate account of those mental states which we need to invoke in order to explain human behaviour, that is, beliefs, etc. – what are often called propositional attitudes in that they have a content which is expressible in a proposition.

It seems implausible to argue that this content is determined simply by the causal origins of the state. A tough-minded functionalist may nevertheless argue that the fact that a mental state has a content is to be explained in terms of some relation that that state has to the other elements of the system to which it belongs, and that differences of content are to be explained in terms of different relations of this sort. In other words, matters of content reduce to matters of the functional role of the state in question. This belief may be encouraged by the thought that the brain is, as Dennett puts it in the paper referred to earlier, a syntactic not a semantic engine. That way of putting the issue is in fact to have recourse to a metaphor. Notions such as those of syntax and semantics apply primarily to language, even if the use and understanding of language presupposes certain forms of mental or psychological competence. Issues about the syntax of language are about its grammatical structure; issues about semantics are issues about how the components of the language have meaning, and in particular how we are enabled by their means to refer to things. To speak, using this metaphor, of the brain as a syntactic engine is to take due note of the fact that, as far as we know (and that qualification is important), the brain works on causal principles which imply structural relations between its elements, between all that and the rest of the nervous system and, because of that, between it and the environment. How does reference to things feature in all that unless it can, improbably perhaps, be reduced to structural considerations?

I say 'improbably perhaps', but those who subscribe to what has been called 'functional role semantics'[8] want to maintain just that reductionist thesis. The motivation for maintaining it is, underneath, ideological, since only if such a reduction can be carried out is it obvious how the workings of the mind can be explained in purely causal terms. Arguably, it involves not taking intentionality seriously, or at least maintaining the possibility of intentionality being reduced in all respects that matter for psychology to something else. In that case, the thesis that intentionality involves something special about the mind would become irrelevant. To have a belief, for example, would be simply to be in a state where all that matters is the role that that state plays in the general economy of the mind; that too would be all that the content of the belief (which is what individuates it) comes to. In the sense of the metaphor used by Dennett, semantics would be reduced to syntax. Functional role semantics has plenty of adherents but in its generality it constitutes merely a programme. Just how it would work out in detail is difficult to see. If it involves not taking intentionality seriously, and therefore not taking seriously what many philosophers have thought essential to belief and analogous mental states, it remains a somewhat curious account of how what is to be understood by beliefs is to be spelled out in functional terms. For it does not really perform the reduction that is called for; it merely presents a programme as to how on certain assumptions it *might* be performed. But it is the assumptions themselves that are questionable.

Suppose, however, that we take seriously the idea of intentionality as involving a notion of content or 'aboutness' which is not reducible in the ways contemplated. Does there remain any possibility of maintaining a sort of functionalism? According to Fodor's flow-chart, yes. For his own theory, the so-called representational theory of the mind (RTM), is on his account just that. It is to be noted, however, that this also entails taking folk psychology extremely seriously as far as inner states are concerned (although less attention is paid in this respect to input and output, which, if I am right, queers the pitch). For he starts from what he describes as a realist position on propositional attitudes and one that takes what is involved in them, that is, their intentionality in the sense set out, seriously. The flow-chart, together with his commentary on it, leads, in his view, to the representational theory of the mind as the only viable possibility. Before we can examine that claim, however, we need to look at the idea of mental representations in general. To this I turn in my next section.

REPRESENTATIONS

The notion of representations is not confined to the RTM. It has become a commonplace in cognitive psychology in general and not merely in that particular branch of cognitive science. How it came to have that status as a matter of history is not altogether clear. It is likely that it originated in Chomsky's claim that knowledge of the deep structure of language is something with which we are born. For on that assumption there is already written into the brain what is necessary for that knowledge. In that sense it is common for those working in this area to speak of a grammar being represented in the brain. All that this need mean, however, is what I have said – that all that is necessary for knowledge of the grammar is there already in the brain. It might be suggested in addition that the structure of what takes place in the brain must somehow match the structure of the beliefs which make up the knowledge in question. Such a suggestion is quite acceptable as long as not too much is read into the term 'match', as long as it means only that there is some correspondence between the two. A strict theory of matching might amount to a thesis of isomorphism similar to that which I noted earlier in my brief discussion of Gestalt Psychology, and there are no grounds for thinking that theory true. All that is required of a theory of matching in the present context is that there should be a law-like correspondence between brain states and items of belief, knowledge, or whatever it is that we are seeking to explain in cortical terms.

Some might argue that even that is too large a concession and that we have no right simply to assume mental–physical parallel-ism in this way. Moreover, even if we make the assumption all the same, there is what Wittgenstein called the myth of the mental process, the myth that when we speak of someone believing that p, remembering that p, etc., there is always some identifiable mental process taking place which is distinct for each case of believing, remembering, etc.[9] There is no single thing that is believing that p; it depends on what p means for the person concerned, what other beliefs he has and so on. So much is the last true that it can be argued that the idea of a single belief standing by itself, an atomic belief so to speak, and more particu-larly the idea of a being with a single belief at any stage, is literally unintelligible. One must therefore proceed very carefully with the idea of a matching relation between beliefs and brain states, and the same applies to other so-called intentional states, such as desires. To speak of them as being represented in the brain equally requires careful examination before acceptance. There is even virtue in approaching the suggestion itself with some scep-ticism.

Even if there were a definite matching between brain states and whatever is said to be represented in the brain, this would not be enough to justify the assertion that we must accept the existence of representations whether cortical or mental. One can see this by considering cases of items between which there is a clear and definite matching – for example, an object and its reflection in a mirror, or, to invoke an example from Plato's *Theaetetus* which has a certain relevance to our concerns, a seal and its impression on a wax tablet. We should not ordinarily speak of a reflection in a mirror as a representation of what is reflected, and if we might speak of the impression in the wax as a representation of the pattern on the seal this is for the special reason that we may for certain purposes treat it in that way. When I say that we should not ordinarily speak in this way I do not simply make an appeal to ordinary language as if that in itself demands our acceptance. It is not an accidental or contingent fact that we do not speak in this way; more is required of a representation than mere similarity to its object.[10]

Let us consider further Plato's use of the example of the wax and the seal. The context in which it is used is the attempt to explain how false belief is possible, in spite of expectations to the contrary when a certain conception of knowledge is assumed, that is, the conception that knowledge requires the presence of the object clearly before the mind such that the only alternative is for it not to be before the mind at all. Plato sees a particular difficulty in the idea of the *mis*identification of someone. If I have someone clearly before my mind, how can I confuse him with someone else? Whereas, if I don't have him before my mind at all, I shall not be in the position to do anything with regard to him, let alone confuse him with someone else. The model of the wax and the seal is adduced in order to explain the possibility of at least one kind of misidentification. (It does not touch the initial problem, but no matter.) It is supposed that perception is like the impressing of the seal on a wax tablet, leaving an impression on it. When I perceive a person at a later stage the seal will be matched with an already existing impression, and error will occur if the seal is matched to the wrong impression. As a model for perceptual recognition and mis-recognition, it is crude, but as will become apparent later certain modern accounts of these matters are not far from it.

The point that I wish to make is that, in the process of identifying or misidentifying something as another thing previously perceived, the impression previously formed can well be regarded as a representation of the object. It might be argued that that is because we treat it in that way, as we do, for example, pictures or sketches of objects or scenes. Plato's account is somewhat ambiguous or indeterminate in this respect. For it to fit the suggestion just made, it would have to be the case that the matching is one which *we* perform, by comparing the impression with the perceived object. It is not entirely clear whether Plato intends that, and we need not for present purposes read it into his account. It would be sufficient if we regarded the model as one of the mechanisms which make identification or misidentification of things possible. That is to say that we might explain the identification or misidentification of objects in terms of some matching process carried out by our nervous system, as a result of which we are enabled to identify an object as one previously seen, with occasional errors. In that case the function of the impression, in relation to the identification of objects by us, is to act as a representation of the object previously perceived, and it is for that reason, but only for that reason, that it can be regarded as a representation. If it had no such function it could not rightly be regarded as a representation at all, and it is because mirror images normally have no such function that it is not right to consider them as representations. (I say 'normally' because it is conceivable that they could in certain circumstances be given that function by intention, just as is the case with pictures designed as representations of objects.[11])

Mental images may be regarded as representations in the same way. It is not that they always *are* representations; for an image may occur to us which is not *of* anything. But in the context of some train of thought an image may clearly function as a representation of something. There is a dispute in the psychological literature between proponents of 'propositional' theories of such representation and 'analogue' theories of it. The chief participants in this dispute are S. M. Kosslyn on the one side and Z. W. Pylyshyn on the other, although A. V. Paavio ought also to be mentioned in this connection.[12] The underlying question at stake is whether images function in the context of propositionally styled thought, whether in Pylyshyn's language they are cognitively penetrable and so determined by beliefs, etc., or whether they are used simply as constructions of an imagined scene. The experimental evidence seems to point in both directions and this is hardly surprising. Many philosophers too have wanted to argue against the thesis that images are pictures in the mind, as against other philosophers who have argued to the contrary. The fact that the evidence is two-sided is not surprising, because the status of an image may depend on the role that it plays in our mental life generally, and there is more than one such role. To the extent that imagining a scene is a matter of constructing in our mind in quasi-perceptual form what we know or believe about the scene, the images involved will be 'cognitively penetrable'; but that does not undermine the possibility that images may have, so to speak, a life of their own, as a result of which we may be able to learn, from a consideration of them, something about the features of the objects of which they are images, just as we may learn similar things from after-images. (That possibility is even more obviously available for those capable of eidetic imagery.) Given that duality in the role of images, the conflicting experimental results may well be a product of the conflicting natures of the experimental set-ups and the designs of the experimenters.

However that may be, it may become clear from these considerations in what way or ways mental images can be considered as representations. They are certainly that if they are used to represent a scene, and they may function in that way in certain cognitive contexts. But in either case they serve as representations *for us*; that is to say that they function in such a way that they have the significance for us that representational pictures normally have for us. Moreover, they can be used in certain cognitive tasks in a way that, say, photographs may be used to make sense of a scene and enable us to answer questions about it. But for something to have a significance for us in this way intentionality on our part must already be presumed. That is what Pylyshyn is in effect saying when he asserts that images are cognitively penetrable. Whatever their exact role in relation to trains of thought or other cognitive exercises, if they have significance for us they must have some such role. It follows that we cannot appeal to images as representations to explain how intentionality functions, since their representational role presupposes intentionality, and to reinvoke representations to explain that would generate an infinite regress. The same will apply to anything which has the same epistemic status.

We have now surveyed two cases where there may be a matching relation between something and something else. In the first case, the mirror image, there is no reason, despite the matching, to think of it as in any significant sense a representation. In the second, there exists both some form of matching and something which in a given context fulfils a representational function, in that whatever it is functions in such a way that it has the significance which a representation, such as a picture, normally has for us. But we have not met with anything which plays what one might call a *naturally* representational role, such that one might appeal to it in order to explain intentionality. Indeed, the examples of representations which I have noted so far all *presuppose* intentionality, so that they cannot be used to explain it. I emphasize this point because, as the notion of representations is used in the RTM, representations are appealed to in order to explain intentionality, and they do appear to constitute things which are supposed to have a natural representational role.

It has been suggested to me that one might simply adopt the word 'representation' to refer to any state with a semantic content, such that operations might be performed on it which are equally semantic or logical. The difficulty with this suggestion is that it merely shifts the problem to the idea of a state which has semantic content. It might be suggested that this is just what beliefs are – they are states and they have a content. I shall have more to say about beliefs later in this chapter, but it is surely wrong to think of beliefs as states which have content just like that, independent of other things about the believer and what they mean to him or her. The issue here is not whether beliefs have content which is natural as opposed to conventional; it is one of whether beliefs have content in their own right and independently of the part that they play in the life of the believer. Hence, when I speak of whether something can have a naturally representational role, that is what I mean.

Before considering these matters further it is necessary to give some attention to certain additional points about the notion of representation as it is used in the cognitive science area. In what I have said so far I have not been very explicit about what such representations are representations *of*. Indeed, in speaking of the use of 'representation' in connection with Chomsky I spoke of knowledge of grammar being represented in the brain without making explicit whether it is what one might call the state of knowing (if there is any such thing) which is so represented there or what is known, that is, in this case, the grammar. In the case of images considered as representations there is no such ambiguity. One psychologist who relies heavily on the notion of representations, David Marr, speaks as follows:[13] 'A *representation* is a formal system for making explicit certain entities or types of information, together with a specification of how the system does this.' There are many problems about this formulation.

There is, first, the fact that the disjunction 'entities or types of information' seems to disjoin two very different kinds of thing, although this by itself may not constitute an objection. We are subsequently told that various numeral systems are all formal systems for representing numbers. Do they make numbers explicit and are numbers entities or what? Second, it is claimed that a representation involves also a specification of how the system makes these things explicit. If this formulation were to be taken at its face value it would have the consequence that a numeral system could not constitute a representation of numbers. For a numeral system as such does not contain rules for its own application, although it undoubtedly presupposes such rules for its application. Later (p. 21), having given other examples of representations – musical scores and alphabets – Marr says: 'To say that something is a formal scheme means only that it is a set of symbols with rules for putting them together – no more and no less.' But that still leaves the question whether the rules are in fact part of the representation or not. It is certainly not adequate to claim that what is said deals with the matter, 'no more and no less'. (There is an additional point that it seems better to speak of such things as numeral systems and musical scores as modes or ways of representing what they present rather than as representations themselves; but I shall not press that point, although the point is analogous to the one which I made about the use of 'behaviours' in an earlier chapter.)

The situation over the use of 'representation' is not helped by the fact that some other writers in this area speak of the representation of rules themselves. Daniel Dennett does this, for example,[14] although, as the title of his paper makes clear, he is concerned primarily with *mental* representations in a way which makes his central concern the use of 'representation' within the RTM. Nevertheless, some of the points that arise in this connection have some generality. Dennett is concerned to make a distinction between explicit (as opposed to implicit) representation and tacit representation. The whole point of making this distinction is to make it possible to think, in terms of representations, of the ability to act in accordance with rules without these being spelled out on each occasion of their use. In this spirit, Dennett can happily ask (and answer) the question whether the rules of arithmetic are represented in a calculator, it being presumed that the computing analogy can validly be applied to the mental processes of human beings. If nothing else is clear, it is surely clear that one cannot speak of the rules of arithmetic being explicitly represented in calculators. To the extent that the brain-processes of human beings work in analogous computational ways the same must apply in their case too.

However that may be, we now seem to have a number of different possible objects of representations – entities of various kinds, information, knowledge and rules. What surely unites these candidates for the title of 'object of a representation' is that the appeal to representations is meant to explain how it is possible for them to be *known*. What we are in effect being told is that knowledge of them is not possible unless there is in us some coded version of such knowledge in the way in which there may be such in a computer (in which, it should be noted again, there is stored both data and the rules for the processing of the data). Dennett's almost formal statement of what explicit representation is is as follows:

> Let us say that information is represented *explicitly* in a system if and only if there actually exists in the functionally relevant place in the system a physically structured object, a *formula* or *string* or *tokening* of some members of a system (or 'language') of elements for which there is a semantics or interpretation, and a provision (a mechanism of some sort) for reading or parsing the formula. (p. 216)

Tacit representation is said to occur when what is done by a system is analogous to what is done by a system as spelled out above without there being any explicit representation as so defined.

But what is it for a system to be such that its elements have a semantics or interpretation when the rules for this are not a matter of what they are for us, as they are in the case of numeral systems, scores, alphabets and maps? For if such a system is to be realized in a brain its elements must have a semantic function naturally and independently, not merely relative to the epistemic life of the believer. It is indeed Dennett's sensitivity to this or a similar point which in part makes him take an instrumentalist attitude to these matters, so that he does not have to assume in a realistic way any form of natural semantics. With *that* idea we are back to what I said earlier about the difficulty inherent in the idea of a natural representation. It is impossible to see what a natural representational system would be, if by that is meant a system which is representational in its own right, without any appeal to the role that it plays relative to a possessor of intentionality, relative, as I have said, to the epistemic (and, as we shall see, other) life of the believer. If that is so, how can we appeal to such a thing in order to explain anything that involves intentionality? All that we have really got so far is that if intentionality is to be possible there must be something in the brain that makes it possible. Such a thesis is obviously empty unless more content can be given to the notion of a representation as a foundation for the notion of intentionality.

THE REPRESENTATIONAL THEORY OF THE MIND

The RTM claims to give the justification demanded at the end of the last section for the use of the notion of representations as a foundation for the notion of intentionality. Indeed, as Fodor presents the theory it is the existence and nature of propositional attitudes, such as belief and desire, which, in his view, necessitate an appeal to representations.[15] This view demands, of course, and this is explicitly recognized by Fodor, the acceptance of at least this part of folk psychology – but is it not clear to most of us that we do have beliefs and desires?

One of the clearest presentations of the issues in this respect is to be found in at least the opening pages of a well-known article by Hartry Field entitled 'Mental representation'.[16] Field starts from what he calls, advisedly, 'Brentano's problem' – advisedly because, as we have seen, it is Brentano who originated the problem of intentionality in modern times. However, Field characterizes the problem as one of giving a materialistically adequate account of believing, desiring and so forth. This is a very different account of the problem from the one which Brentano presented, since Brentano insisted that belief and so forth belong to a range of mental acts which, because of their intentionality (the necessity of their having an intentional object which has *inesse* in relation to them), have characteristics which nothing material has. By contrast Field claims that Brentano thought the problem (though as construed by Field) insoluble.

Field takes materialism as unquestionably true; so the problem is how there can be anything, given that assumption, which has intentionality. The answer, Field thinks, lies in some sort of appeal to the notion of mental representation, in that belief (and other propositional attitudes, which are so called because they have a content to be expressed in propositional terms and some sort of mental relation to that content) must be analysed in terms of a relation to an *object*. That is to say that the fact that the propositional attitude has a content is to be explained only by the assumption that there is in it a relation to an object. That object is not necessarily an objective state of affairs, since beliefs can be false and desires unrealizable; it must, however, be propositional. Field eventually concludes that the relation of belief to propositions can itself be explained only in terms of the idea that belief entails a system of internal representations.

The problems raised by the possibility of false belief for an adequate account of what belief is have a long philosophical history, going back at least to Plato. Sometimes attempts have been made to construe belief (and of course the same would have to apply, *mutatis mutandis*, to other propositional attitudes) in non-relational terms, so that there need be no question of bringing in any object extrinsic to the belief state. The obvious problem about this derives from the fact that beliefs can be true or false, and which they are depends on factors independent of the state of mind. It is therefore hard to see how one could give an adequate account of belief without bringing in something about things in the world or at least things independent of the belief. As we shall see later, what appear to be similar considerations have been raised, by, for example, Putnam, in connection with meaning. As Putnam puts it, meanings 'ain't in the head'. These considerations have been taken further, by, for example, Tyler Burge, so as to argue that at least some cases of meaning involve social considerations. I shall myself argue that social considerations enter via the notion of truth itself, and that this notion is presupposed not only by knowledge and belief, but by meaning itself.

Attempts have also been made by, for example, Russell[17] to analyse belief purely in terms of a relation between the believer and objects independent of the believer, so that there need be no reference to internal objects of any kind. Thus Russell suggested that Othello's belief that Desdemona loved Cassio could be analysed in terms of a many-termed relation between Othello, Desdemona, loving and Cassio. Such a relation might hold whether or not Desdemona did love Cassio, although since loving is one of the terms of the relation and there are questions to be raised about what sort of term that can be, the relation in question is not entirely unproblematic. Russell indeed came to see it as problematic in another way, in that it matters for the belief whether it is a matter of Desdemona loving Cassio or

Cassio loving Desdemona, and these possibilities are not distinguished by speaking of a many-termed relation as he had done. Loving is in fact a relation itself, and in spelling it out the sense or direction of the relation must be preserved. So, in his 'The philosophy of logical atomism',[18] Russell insisted on the importance of the word 'that' in the formulation of a belief attribution, so recognizing the necessarily propositional character of a belief. He maintained indeed that in respect of the task of providing an analysis of types of proposition we have in belief propositions a 'new beast for the zoo'. Similarly Frege had earlier maintained that the reference of the that-clause in a belief statement was the sense of the proposition involved, not its reference, which would be a truth-value.[19]

One way of putting that would be to say that the object of a belief is a proposition. It might be said of course that one believes all sorts of things – sometimes the facts, sometimes what one reads in the paper, sometimes what people tell one, sometimes what one has found out by inquiry, and so on. When one asks what is the object of belief one is not really asking a question which demands answers of those kinds. What is being asked is what it is, if the state of belief is in some sense relational, that the belief, considered in general, is related to? The answer 'Propositions' brings out that belief has a content expressible in propositions. But it is impossible to think of the reference to those propositions as simply giving an intrinsic characterization of the belief state. If that was how it is, it would be difficult to explain what it is to believe and desire the same thing, or for different people to believe the same thing, and so on. Yet it is also impossible to hold that belief involves simply a relation to the facts, because beliefs can be false, and when they are they do not have a relation to the facts. It is of course for analogous reasons that Brentano thought that belief, or rather judgement, involved a direction of the mind to an intentional object, which has being only in relation to the belief, but such that there is no real relation between the mind and any existent thing.

But that sort of view is just the view which leads Field to say that Brentano thought his problem insoluble – because if belief is a relational state it ought to involve a relation to something actual. Do propositions fit the bill in this respect? What are they, and are they something actual? Whole hosts of recent philosophers, from G. E. Moore onwards, have thought the reference to propositions unsatisfactory, and many of them have looked for a more promising candidate, something actual, for that to which the belief state is directed. The most likely candidate, at any rate for the tough-minded, is sentences; for they are at all events actually existing things. They can be written down, recorded, seen, heard, and so on. But which sentences in particular are we related to when we believe that p or that q? I do not mean by that question to ask that a type sentence (any sentence to the effect that p or that q) be provided by way of an answer. I ask what token sentence or sentences we are related to in having those beliefs. It might be argued (and I believe that I have heard Davidson argue) that there might be some token sentence to which one is related in these contexts, but that one does not have to know which. It is hard to know what to make of such a suggestion. Can it be the case that when one believes that it is a fine day, to have that belief is to stand in some kind of relation to some token sentence to that effect without necessarily knowing which? Failing that thought, it is necessary to identify the sentence in question. And how is that to be done?

One possible way of doing that, it is suggested (and it is a view which in effect embraces the RTM), is to suppose that when one believes p one is related to an internal sentence, which might have a realization in some brain state. Such a sentence would be one which is, in Fodor's terms, a sentence in the language of thought. It would involve what Dennett has termed more critically 'brain writing'.[20] Such constituents of the language of thought, so called, amount to the representations which are the crucial feature of the RTM. It is this which Field is talking about when he refers to mental representation. Such representations, like sentences in general, have both a syntax and a semantics, and, as we have seen, the argument for their existence stems from considerations about intentionality in general and propositional attitudes in particular.

The idea that thought involves inner speech, and that there is in that sense anything like the language of thought has been rejected by Wittgenstein and those inspired by him, although the idea that thought, including propositional attitudes such as belief, involves the soul talking to itself is to be found as early as Plato.[21] The idea of the language of thought as presupposed by the RTM is somewhat different from that, since its sentences are not objects for a thinking subject. They are, nevertheless, *objects* presupposed in virtue of the relational character of belief and other intentional states. As most of the writers concerned with the RTM present the issues, the rationale of the need to posit representations and thereby, because such representations have a propositional character, the language of thought, stems from such issues about intentionality. The sentences of the language of thought, so called, constitute representations because they have a semantics as well as a syntax; they relate in some way to the world and it is in virtue of this that they are true or false.

If, however, one approaches the issues in this way (that is, by starting from beliefs and other propositional attitudes and asking how the conditions for their possible existence are to be satisfied) there is inevitably a problem how the so-called representations which are posited can have the representational character that they are supposed to have. At the end of his paper on 'Propositional attitudes' Fodor says:

> If the representational theory of the mind is true, then we know what propositional attitudes are. But the net total of philosophical problems is surely not decreased thereby. We must now face what has always been *the* problem for representational theories to solve: what relates internal representations to the world? What is it for a system of internal representations to be semantically interpreted? I take it that this problem is now the main content of the philosophy of mind.

This states the issues well enough. In other papers Fodor has gestured towards an answer to his question. At the end of his 'Methodological solipsism considered as a research strategy for cognitive psychology'[22] he (jokingly?) suggests that 'truth, reference and the rest of the semantic notions aren't psychological categories. What they are is: they're modes of *Dasein*.' And he adds: 'I don't know what *Dasein* is, but I'm sure that there's lots of it around, and I'm sure that you and I and Cincinnati have all got it. What more do you want?'[23]

Unfortunately, the answer to that last question must be 'A great deal'. In one way indeed the reference to *Dasein* is rather unfortunate. It is presumably a reference to Heidegger's use of that term to speak of 'being in the world', and what Fodor probably has in mind is some causal story about our relations with the world. But for Heidegger *Dasein* is not a form of being in the world that anything can have; it is the unique way of being in the world which human beings, but not other kinds of thing, have. So the joke misfires. At the end of 'Fodor's guide to mental representation' he admits that 'of the semanticity of mental representations we have, as things now stand, no adequate account' and refers to a possible glimpse of a causal/teleological theory of meaning, the development of which 'would provide a way out of the current mess'. But that is just a hope, or, as a more severe critic might say, a piece of wishful thinking.

Nevertheless, Fodor adheres to what he calls, as in the title of the paper referred to above, 'methodological solipsism'. The term was introduced by Carnap, but in Fodor's use of it it implies what is said in the quotation from the paper given above – that reference to the world is not a psychological category, it is not a matter for psychology. On this view, the psychology of an individual must involve only what holds good of that individual, and for Fodor that means the representations which make up the individual's mind, and to which computational principles apply. To put the matter in other terms, only a narrow conception of content must be presupposed by a scientific psychology.[24] What is generally contrasted with this view in contemporary literature is the view stemming from Putnam's paper 'The meaning of "meaning"'[25] to the effect that meanings 'ain't in the head'. Putnam's argument, which has attained something of the status of a *locus classicus*, depends on a twin-earth thought experiment. The thought is that there might be a twin-earth on which there was a stuff perceptually indistinguishable from water on earth but in fact having a quite different composition. Someone on earth and a twin-earther might both refer to the water-like substance as water, but *ex hypothesi* they would be referring to stuff of a quite different nature. So what they would mean by 'water' would be different, and it is taken to follow from that that 'meanings ain't in the head'. Tyler Burge[26] has extended the argument to show that social as well as physical contexts may affect what someone may mean, since the meaning of certain terms in which beliefs may be expressed and attributed may vary according to social context.

An acceptance of these arguments ought to entail the acceptance of the view that a full story of the cognitive psychology of an individual must extend beyond that individual. There may also be other arguments of different kinds which lead to the same conclusion.[27] The question that remains is what consequences this must be taken to have for the RTM. For it is very unclear what bearing it has on the argument that directly leads to the RTM – the relational character of belief and the fact that beliefs cannot always be taken to have the facts as their object. For it may be argued that when someone believes that p, then, whatever p amounts to, some representation is involved; whether it is properly to be described as a representation having the semantic content that p may depend on factors extrinsic to it, but it nevertheless remains the case that in explaining, for example, a person's behaviour by reference to, among other things, that belief one will be implying the existence of a representation to which *on this occasion and in this context* is to. be attributed the semantic content that p.

Nevertheless, some, for example, Stich,[28] have taken these considerations, or ones like them, as indicating that the notion of belief should have no place in a scientific psychology. Basically the argument is that these considerations about belief offend against the principle that only current, physical properties are relevant to explanatory psychological properties, and that if two human beings are psychologically identical then 'any psychological property instantiated by one of these subjects will also be instantiated by the other' (*The Monist*, 1978, p. 574). This is termed by Stich the principle of psychological autonomy. The basis of the principle, which is also discussed by Fodor in 'Individualism and supervenience', is that each human being ought to be considered as, so to speak, a psychological atom, and that nowhere else in science do the properties of an atom depend on the properties of other things, even if atoms do stand in relations to other things. To maintain such a view, however, is in effect to beg the question of what is appropriate to psychology and simply assumes that all psychological properties are locally supervenient on physical ones – and thus *assumes* a position on the body–mind problem.

For all that, Fodor's question 'What relates internal representations to the world?' also remains and is not answered by any of the considerations surveyed. Or at all events it remains if he is right that an analysis of propositional attitudes demands reference to internal representations. For that question is not so much the question of the circumstances under which a representation of X is a representation of X but the question how something can be an internal representation at all. How is it possible for it to represent?

There are two important things which must be noted about all this. There is, first, the point which I have just been considering. But it arises, first and foremost, because Fodor in effect starts from internal states – states which have the character of sentences in the so-called language of thought. He starts from that point because he accepts what is supposed to be the received doctrine about folk psychology – that behaviour receives its explanation by reference to beliefs and desires, both of which constitute intentional states. I am not here concerned to dispute this 'received doctrine', although I do not think that all behaviour is explicable by reference to combinations of belief and desire as the official paradigm suggests. The point which I wish to make here is that it is supposed that behaviour, construed as the output of a system which is physically realizable, can be explained only in terms of internal states which are similarly realizable. It is then naturally a problem how these states can have reference to the world external to the system – how the brain can function as a semantic engine, in Dennett's language.

Little is said in all this about how the input and output ought to be conceived if they are to be related by reference to beliefs and desires. We shall see later if the situation is any better when we have given proper consideration to these matters, but it ought to be apparent now that Dennett's question about how the brain can be a semantic engine is likely to remain on any event. But this is not, as Fodor suggests, the problem which 'is now the main content of the philosophy of mind'. The main content of the philosophy of mind ought to be an adequate account of mental concepts themselves. How they are realized in physical terms is perhaps a version of the mind–body problem, but it is no good assuming that the physical processes work in certain ways and that the mental concepts have to fit that. As I have said, perhaps we shall be clearer on the concepts themselves when a more adequate account of input and output have been given.

The second point is that it is assumed, in all the considerations which lead to the RTM, that beliefs are states with a straightforward content of the kind which makes reference to representations as their objects plausible. Is it the case, however, that beliefs (and the same will apply to other putative intentional states) are states in the sense here presupposed? I mentioned in the previous chapter the point that beliefs presuppose *attitudes* on our part. It is arguable also that they presuppose *knowledge* – a point to which I shall return – and this too may have some consequences for our present position. The point on which I wish to concentrate at present, however, is one about their identity conditions. Does the idea of a representation, as something given the content of whatever processes take place in belief, suffice to identify a state as a belief? I shall try to consider this question and its implications in the next section.

THE INDIVIDUATION OF BELIEFS

What I have to say in this section will be put in terms of beliefs, but it has equal relevance to anything to which intentionality applies, that is, whenever the so-called state of mind is specified by reference to an object which need not correspond to anything in the world. It is natural to think that a belief is individuated by reference to the proposition which gives in this way its content, so that the criterion of identity for beliefs is given by their object or content so specified. In a way that is right. Two people may be said to have the same belief that p if they both believe that p – and no more needs to be said. But the implications for X and Y of their sharing the same belief in this way may be very different in each case. For X may know things relevant to p that Y does not know or vice versa; they may understand what is entailed by p differently, and so on. Moreover, in many cases, perhaps all, having one belief, specified as the belief that p, entails and presupposes having a number of other beliefs. One cannot believe, for example, that Henry VIII had six wives without believing that there was a king called 'Henry VIII', that he was married, that he was married more than once, that there is an institution of marriage, that there are wives, that six is a number, and so on. But the 'and so on' is important, as is equally the fact of what exactly is understood by the terms which I have used in specifying the beliefs in question. Someone who believes also that Henry

VIII, or the Henry VIII in question, was a French king, or a Stuart king, inevitably has a belief to the effect that Henry VIII had six wives which is in many ways different from that of someone who knows the facts, even if there is also a sense in which they have the same belief.

All this undermines the view that the identification of a belief *considered as a belief state* is provided simply by the specification of its content. It equally undermines the view that there is any obvious way of counting beliefs. There is no saying how many beliefs a person has when he or she believes that p. It will be remembered that according to Fodor's thesis in *The Modularity of Mind* central processes are Quinean and isotropic. To say that they are Quinean is to say that they cannot be broken down into atomic elements and to say that they are isotropic is to say that anything from any domain may be relevant to what is being considered. The Quinean thesis from which this is derived, however, is one about the verification or falsification of propositions according to their status within a theory.[29] Moreover, the relevance which is at stake within the thesis of isotropy is one which has to do with the determination of truth. These theses are not directly about content as providing identity conditions for belief, unless it is held that meaning or content has directly to do with determination of truth, unless, that is, meaning is a matter of verification.

The same is true of another thesis in this area – Davidson's thesis of the holism of the mental.[30] According to that thesis it is impossible to determine a person's beliefs independently of the determination of his desires, and vice versa. This is because in relation to his behaviour we can ascribe a belief to that person only if we know what he desires and vice versa. But, as that way of putting the matter indicates, the issue is about the verification of certain propositions about a person's beliefs and desires, given the facts about his behaviour. It might be that such verification is impossible *because* beliefs do not exist independent of desires and vice versa. But that conclusion does not follow from any considerations about having to appeal to both beliefs and desires together in order to explain a person's behaviour.

Both Fodor's 'Quinean' thesis and Davidson's thesis about the holism of the mental are, therefore, theses about our determination of someone's beliefs; they are not, directly, theses about the actual nature of beliefs. But the thesis that there is no saying how many beliefs a person has when he believes that p *is* a thesis about the nature of beliefs. For it involves the claim that, apart from the simple reference to content, what it is to believe that p is, within limits, essentially indeterminate. There have to be some limits on this; otherwise the belief that p would not be distinguishable from any other belief, and it would not make sense to speak of different people having the same belief. But, whatever may be the evidence for this in their case, the only certain identification of the belief itself is via its content; and this has no definite implications for what else in particular must be true of the persons concerned. Hence, as I have previously said, what holds good of a person when he or she believes that p is indeterminate, and there is no escaping that fact. There is not just one state that is the state of believing that p.

A further point that seems to emerge from all this is that there is no such state as one belief independent of other beliefs. Believing that S is P entails knowing in some way what S and P are (or in other words, having the concepts of S and P, which is, in my view, to be elucidated in terms of the idea of knowledge). Whatever general thesis be held about the relation between knowledge and belief, whether, that is, knowledge that p always entails the belief that p, it would seem very odd to say that someone could know what it is for something to be S or P without having any beliefs on these matters. It is at the very least a plausible thesis that there are no atomic beliefs, no beliefs that can be held without holding any other beliefs. Furthermore, if to believe that p is to believe that p is true, and if that entails knowing what it is for something to be true, then no belief can be held without there being also some belief about what it is for something to be true. It appears, therefore, that any one belief will bring with it a complex web of other beliefs.[31]

If it be accepted that one cannot have one belief without having others, in that one belief specified in terms of its content (as the belief that p, for example) presupposes other beliefs, certain other things follow. First, the relation between one belief and the others in the web of belief is not just a semantic relation; it is not merely a relation depending on the relations between the contents of the beliefs. The holding of one belief presupposes at least *assent* to others, and that means that the relation between them is epistemic, rather than merely semantic. The question of what else someone believes when he believes that p is a question, not merely of what he understands by p (and we have noted already how indeterminate that may be), but of what else he is committed to in believing that p. This rises directly from the fact that, as we noted earlier, belief involves certain attitudes to what is believed, particularly attitudes to its truth or falsity.

One further point can be made in this connection. I have suggested (without making much of a meal of it) that belief presupposes knowledge. But knowledge is something which admits of degrees. One may know something better than someone else may do; it is possible to know something to a greater extent than one may know something else; one can know more things about one thing than one may know about another. Belief itself admits of degrees, of course, in that it may be subject to varying degrees of conviction, but that is a matter of differences in the attitude, the commitment, involved in the belief, rather than, as is the case with the point about knowledge, a matter of variations in extent in the object, variations of degree in what is known. Nevertheless, the fact that knowledge admits of degrees in this way affects what is involved in the belief that p. Knowledge is not an either/or matter; as a consequence the determinacy of the state which constitutes a belief is affected, not only by the varying degrees of understanding of what is involved on the part of the believer, and on the varying commitments in that regard, but also by the varying amounts of what is known by him that is relevant to the belief.[32]

That belief is dispositional is a familiar thesis among philosophers,[33] for the evidence for a belief is often a matter of what the person concerned is disposed to do and say. It is equally true that other philosophers have not been willing to leave matters at that, asserting that a disposition must have a categorical base.[34] What emerges from the considerations here adduced is that whatever categorical base there is for the belief that p cannot be in all cases a single state of mind which is realizable in a single brain state, although it must surely be that whenever X believes that p there is *some* brain state which holds good of him. Nor is it plausible, in consequence, to suppose that the belief that p is to be construed in terms of a set of computational processes directed to a single internal representation or even a determinate set of representations. But without that supposition RTM has little plausibility or attractiveness. The supposition that there must be brain states which have something to do with the fact that our beliefs are *about* things is obviously valid, but that is not to say that any of these function as representations. A belief involves much more than that.

Before I leave this particular matter, there is perhaps one further point to be made. There is little attempt on the part of exponents of the RTM to explain how representations come about. It is assumed that transducers transform the pattern of physical energy that is set up by stimulation of sense-organs into something which is information bearing, so as to be subject to computational processes. Hence representations. Any solution to the problem of the so-called semantics of these representations (and the use of the term 'semantics' clearly involves a metaphor, by which the reference of representations to the world is likened to the way in which language gains meaning by reference) must be found in the causal processes by which they are set up. It is difficult to see how that is to be done, however, and that is a further reason why it may be tempting for adherents of the theory to maintain, as Fodor in effect does, that the representations are already there and are merely 'triggered off' by the causal processes in question. Thus, on Fodor's view, all concepts (which are, in his view, a species of representation) are either innate or derived from those which are innate by computational processes. But even perception itself must equally be a form of triggering on this view; for the transducers which transform physical energy into information are built into the system. This is a revival of Plato's theory of recollection, according to which all perception involves a triggering off of knowledge previously obtained. It is surprising to find a theory almost universally thought grossly implausible revived in this way.

Nevertheless, if all this baggage is bought and accepted, it may appear that it is unnecessary to inquire further into the nature of perception, construed as an input process. Equally, it may be supposed that all that needs to be said about output is that the central processes then cause behaviour to take place. The nature of the two sets of causal processes – input and output – may then be taken to determine what beliefs can be attributed when it is also known what desires the subject has. We have beliefs, then, and they are the result of computational processes on representations. That view is intelligible, given the computational approach to the mind, or at any rate it may seem so.

It may be thought, in consequence, a subsidiary matter, at the most, to deal with perception, for the input processes seem obviously to involve input systems or transducers, serving to translate what is merely physical into information-bearing states. It may equally seem a subsidiary matter to deal with action or behaviour, since this is merely caused by whatever brain states exist when we have certain complexes of beliefs and desires. It is my suggestion that if one pays more attention to both the input and the output systems one might attain a better view, or at least a different view, of the central processes also. At the end of the day one may be no wiser as to exactly how those processes are realized in physical or physiological terms (for I suspect that the mind–body problem will be with us for some time to come at least), but at any rate one will be on a surer basis for the attempt to attain that understanding. I must now turn, therefore, first to perception and a proper account of the input to the system which we, each of us, comprise; secondly to the way in which the past affects the present state of the system; and finally to how the output must be conceived if it is to be relevant to our understanding of behaviour.

4

Perception I: a Proper View of Input?

THE BACKGROUND

The history of thinking about the nature of perception reveals[1] that there has in the past been a tendency to analyse perception either into sensation, so that perception is construed in terms merely of the receipt of sensations as a result of the stimulation of our sense-organs, or into judgement, so that emphasis is laid upon the judgements which we make about the world in view of the stimulation of our sense-organs. There have been certain exceptions to this rule, of which the eighteenth-century philosopher Thomas Reid was a notable example, but the rule holds good in general. What is true is that any adequate account of perception must allow for, among other things, two things which are brought out by these opposing tendencies, even when they go beyond them – the fact that the stimulation of our sense-organs brings about certain experiences, and the fact that in perception there occurs, in some way by the mediation of those experiences, the bringing of objects of perception under concepts.

Apart from a few thinkers, mainly philosophers, who for particular reasons of their own laid emphasis upon judgement, the main tradition in the nineteenth century was a sensationalist one. That is to say that perception was thought to be a matter of the receipt of a mosaic of sensations which were in the last analysis atomic in character, so that any perceptual experience was held to be a complex of sensations which were, ultimately, simple and not further analysable. The tradition which this way of thinking followed goes back at least to Hume, and his doctrine of simple or atomic impressions, into which all other impressions were analysable. At the end of the nineteenth century there were a number of reactions against this way of thinking.[2]

There is no point in going into the details of these reactions here, but Gestalt Theory, which was perhaps the dominant psychological theory of perception in the first half of the present century, was in fact one of those reactions. It had most in common with the phenomenological movement in philosophy led by Edmund Husserl, as one of the leading figures in the Gestalt movement, Wolfgang Köhler, was to recognize, even if Husserl himself was less willing to acknowledge the fact. Nevertheless, the Gestaltists in general accepted much of the sensationalist way of thinking about perception, denying only that perceptual experience could be broken down into atomic elements or sensations. Hence their emphasis upon 'wholes' or 'Gestalten' in perception. Such facts as are evident in the so-called perceptual constancies, the facts that we tend to perceive things as more nearly the right size, shape and colour than would be expected on the basis of the pattern of stimulation of the sense-organs alone, were explained, not by invoking the correcting function of judgement, as had been done by, for example, Helmholtz, but by reference to the tendency of the processes in perception to maintain 'good Gestalt', that is, to have a holistic character.

GIBSON

During the time in which the Gestalt movement was the dominant European school of psychology, the leading school of thinking in American psychology was that of behaviourism. This had little to say about perception as such, since it presumed that behaviour was brought about by stimuli, and, as we noted in an earlier chapter, the only gloss allowed on this was that complexes of stimuli might amount to a 'situation'. Subsequently, although there were many psychologists working in the field of perception, there were no major advances in the theory of perception until the advent of James J. Gibson. In his first book, The Perception of the Visual World,[3] Gibson claimed to be putting forward a psychophysical theory of perception, which might give the impression that he thought that all that there was to perception was a complex array of sensations, and that all that was required of the psychology of perception was to establish the laws connecting those sensations with properties of the physical stimuli. But he also distinguished between the visual field and the visual world. To give an account of the former was to give an account of what is phenomenologically evident when one considers the nature of the perceptual experience in abstraction from what one knows about the world which produces it. Gibson thought that this corresponds to what many philosophers have had in mind when speaking of sense-data, and that one could get some view of it by trying to see things in perspective and as painters see them – by, for example, screwing up one's eyes. We would then see it 'as if it consisted of areas or patches of colored surface, divided up by contours'. This visual field was supposed to be purely sensory and the connections between it and the properties of stimuli were supposed to be purely psychophysical.

By contrast, Gibson held the visual world to be a world of solid objects perceived as at varying distances and under varying conditions. We see objects against a ground, however, and if we consider the corresponding pattern of the visual field we shall see in it gradients of texture, such that objects near to us correspond to larger segments of that texture than distant objects. There is a similar patterning (though, of course, inverted because of the properties of the lens of the eye) in the stimulation of the retina, and therefore of the so-called 'retinal image', in these circumstances. This connection between, on the one hand, the distance and apparent size of objects, and, on the other hand, the texturing of the visual field led Gibson to say that if retinal stimulation is viewed correctly in this way there is in it all that is necessary to explain the facts of our perception of the world. Gibson was in this clearly concentrating on spatial perception, but the account might be extended to deal with our perception of other aspects of things – or so it is claimed. It is far from obvious, however, that the account is sufficient for its purposes, however much it enlarges our conception of the necessary conditions of perception. For one thing, it seems evident that we have to *learn* to see things as they are.

In any case, in his next book, *The Senses Considered as Perceptual Systems*,[4] Gibson played down the idea of a visual field and in consequence dropped the psychophysical theory of perception also. He retained, however, much of the rest of his thinking on the subject. The crucial concept in the theory was now that of information and the senses were conceived as systems actively seeking for information from the environment. That information is to be found in the 'stimulus array', and it was Gibson's central thesis that all the information necessary for the perception of the world is to be found in the stimulus array, and that there is no need to appeal to concepts or any other 'intellectual process'. The sense of 'information' involved is, Gibson said, that of 'information about', and is not the sense of 'information' involved in so-called 'information theory'.[5] The use of the word 'about' in this context indicates that the use of the term 'information' presupposes intentionality; indeed, the sense of the term as used by Gibson is not far from the sense that the term has in ordinary parlance.

An important aspect of Gibson's theory, however, is that because we move around the world, and because objects themselves often move, the stimulus array and the information contained in it are constantly changing. If we are to perceive a world of objects with an identity over time it is necessary that there should be 'invariants' in that changing sequence of stimulation. It is the detection of such invariants that is the primary goal of the senses considered as perceptual systems. Gibson's claim that, given the notion of information and that of the senses as perceptual systems, there is no need to appeal to any other processes, whether intellectual or not, has seemed to many frankly incredible.[6] Surely, if we are to derive information from what the senses provide us with, the sensory systems involved must depend on causal mechanisms of some kind. We must also have the conceptual apparatus to make sense of the information provided, and must there not be mechanisms which make that possible too?

Gibson sometimes called his theory, in application to vision, a theory of 'ecological optics', because it laid weight on the idea of the relation of the perceiver to the environment in the business of information pick-up. He also claimed that his theory was, epistemologically speaking, a realist one, in that it involved no appeal to anything like sense-data from which inferences are made to the characteristics of the real world; it was in that sense direct and not indirect. It makes no appeal to anything like representations, any more than it presupposes concept-use. On the latter point, as I have already suggested, Gibson is wrong, because the notion of information, as he uses it, itself presupposes the idea of concept-use, although covertly. It does this because we can get no information from anything if we are not in a position to understand it, and understanding involves concepts and their use. On the first point, that his theory involves no appeal to anything like representations, Gibson is right both in his assessment of his theory and in his assertion that perception does not involve an epistemic relationship to entities from which inferences to the world are then made. It is information *about the world* which we pick up through the senses in our commerce with the world. His theory is in that sense correctly termed 'realist'.

In his last book, *The Ecological Approach to Visual Perception*,[7] however, certain pragmatist leanings appear in the theory. That book lays great weight on what Gibson calls 'affordances'. For example, firm surfaces afford support and various substances afford sustenance. Gibson says (p. 140) that 'the affordances of things for an observer are specified in stimulus information'; nevertheless, an affordance is relative to an organism in a way in which the objective properties of things are not. The greater the weight that a theory of ecological optics lays on those things which are ecologically of use for the organism the more the pragmatist leanings inherent in the idea of what is of use take over from the realist point of view. The tendencies in Gibson's last book, written shortly before he died, are in that direction. An affordance is such for the perceiving organism; by contrast, the world is as it is whether or not anything perceives it and is not simply relative to the perceiver. Gibson's second book is on firmer ground in this respect, but neither book and neither theory has any truck with representations.

Gibson is mostly concerned with how we manage to perceive the world correctly. He has much less to do with the circumstances in which perception breaks down; he has much less, that is, to do with illusions. A great deal of the psychology of perception has traditionally had to do with just that, however. It is an important fact that perceptual illusions are of various kinds, and that they do not all receive an explanation in the same way. For the reasons why perception breaks down, in the sense that it fails to give us a correct view of things, are likely to cast light on the factors involved in veridical perception. Indeed it may become apparent that what may seem to be from the point of view of veridical perception a single perceptual skill is nothing of the kind, in that one part of it may break down without the other parts. This is indeed a quite general moral to be derived from the work of those engaged in what has become known as cognitive neuropsychology;[8] for the study of various kinds of brain damage and their effect on various cognitive abilities may indicate that one aspect of a cognitive skill may be destroyed without affecting other aspects, so that the skill in question is revealed as not just a single thing. It might be argued, therefore, that Gibson's comparative lack of concern with illusions and other perceptual breakdowns is to be blind to things which make perception possible, and the absence of which makes perception impossible in one way or another. Even if all the information necessary for perception is there in the stimulus array we should surely be concerned with what makes its derivation and receipt possible.

Many critics have emphasized such points and have not been persuaded by what Gibson has to say about 'affordances' and the relation of these to stimulus information, even if what he says rightly lays weight on the relationship of the organism to its environment as a feature of perception. One particularly severe critic of Gibson is Richard Gregory, who has emphasized the way in which people approach situations which are perceived by them with anticipations as to what the situations will be like – something that often explains why they perceive the situations wrongly on occasion. In consequence, Gregory has claimed that perceptions are hypotheses.[9] They cannot, however, be just that, since the beliefs that we acquire about the world in perception depend on information received, however much the process of information receipt may be helped or hindered by our anticipations as to what the world must be like.

Hence, other people in this area have tried to produce a more comprehensive account of perception, of which these different aspects might be parts. Ulric Neisser, who has been, in some ways, something of a convert to Gibson, and was a member of the same department of psychology, speaks of a 'perceptual cycle', formed of what he calls 'anticipatory schemata', information pick-up, and consequent revised schemata.[10] Cognitive structures lead to information pick-up, which in turn produces a revised cognitive structure, and so on. Clearly this process has to start at some point, and this is a problem to which I shall return, although expressed in somewhat different terms. At all events Neisser agrees with Gregory about the need for the perceiver to bring something to bear upon the process of the pick-up of information from the stimulus array, but perception is on this account neither pure information pick-up nor hypothesis formation.[11]

MARR

More needs to be added to this process of syncretism if a complete account of perception is to be achieved. There has to be, for example, a story about the processes which make it all possible, and this is a story that can be told on more than one level. David Marr, whose book *Vision*[12] is an attempt to explain visual perception of the world in information-processing terms involving computation, distinguishes three levels on which such an account might be provided. At the first level there is a description of 'the abstract computational theory of the device, in which the performance of the device is characterized as a mapping from one kind of information to another, the abstract properties of the mapping are defined precisely, and its appropriateness for the task at hand are demonstrated' (*Vision*, p. 24). We are at this level concerned with the question what function is computed and why. At the second level we are concerned with the implementation of this computational theory, the question of what is the appropriate algorithm for connecting input and output. (As might be expected from what I said in an earlier chapter, Marr puts this in terms of the 'choice of representation for the input and output and the algorithm to be used to transform one into the other'.) At the third level we are concerned with the physical realization of the representations and the algorithm.

There is, in other words, the general question of what kind of relationship exists between input and output, the more specific question of what kind of systematic or rule-governed process could manifest and make good that relationship, and the even more specific question of how that process is to be realized in physical terms. The last is clearly a matter for the physiologist. The first is concerned with the general relationship between one cognitive structure and another which obtains when someone perceives something, so that, as we might say, new information is acquired. It is the second which is concerned with the kind of process which makes that possible. As Marr points out, in a comprehensive account these issues are not totally independent of each other. There might be more than one algorithm which could be used to make the transformation involved in linking input and output, and some algorithms might not be easily realized in the kind of physical structure which actually obtains in physiological systems of perception. Hence the task of the psychologist must be to gain some insight into the kind of computational processes which might make perception possible and to relate them to the facts of the situation in such a way that they provide a plausible explanation of what actually takes place. Thus, what happens at level 2 is taken to link the physical situation with the task to be performed.

It is presumed in all this that what will make information pick-up possible is some kind of computational process. Marr relates his account to that of Gibson with some sympathy towards Gibson. He takes up the point about the detection of invariants, and points out that such detection is an information-processing problem. He also suggests that Gibson has 'vastly underrated the sheer difficulty of such detection'. Hence Gibson's account has to be supplemented by an information-processing story. Perhaps Gibson ought not to have rejected such ideas, though no doubt he would have done so. Others too have pointed out the compatibility between what lies at the basis of Gibson's theory and an information-processing theory, whether or not expressed in computational terms.[13]

There is, however, one point on which, officially at any rate, there must be an incompatibility between Marr's approach and Gibson's. Marr, as was noted in an earlier chapter, is very much wedded to the concept of representations, while Gibson, as I have made clear earlier in this chapter, will have nothing to do with them. Yet in a sense their problem is the same. In perception the eye receives a welter of changing patterns of stimulation on what is in effect a two-dimensional surface. How is it that from all this we come to perceive solid, three-dimensional objects with edges which separate them from other objects and from whatever is their background? Gibson answers that there are invariances in the pattern of information so received. Marr answers in effect that computational processes link the representations set up in the input process with the representations in the output; and in this context the output is the perception of the solid, three-dimensional objects in question. To so perceive them is to have the corresponding representations.

It might be thought that there is an ambiguity in the notions of 'representation' used here, but that is not really so; all the representations in question are 'representations of', and the computational processes transform representations of the patterning of light (in Gibsonian terms, of the stimulus array) into representations of objects. What then is the difference between the two accounts? It is that for Marr to perceive an object just is to have a representation of an object, or at least involves that, while for Gibson it is not and does not. If one asks Gibson what perceiving an object then is, one receives no answer, or at least no answer which involves analysing perception in some other terms, except that perception is the receipt of information by means of perceptual systems. It is obviously important that we should get clear about exactly what perception involves, and I shall turn to that question in the next chapter.

Meanwhile, there are one or two further considerations to which attention must be given. First, it is clear that the main concern of both Gibson and Marr is to explain the possibility of our perception of a world of, as I have put it, solid, three-dimensional objects. There is of course more to the world of which we have perception than this; we perceive things with a great variety of properties and as having a certain identity, for example. For this to be possible we have to bring concepts to bear upon objects. Again, perception has some connection with our beliefs and knowledge about the world; but perceiving is not always believing, and there is a sensuous dimension to perception which does not apply to all belief. At the same time, the epistemic identifications and characterizations of things that perception makes possible is often (always?) dependent on past experience, and in a variety of ways. Hence there is much more to perception than the identification of solid, three-dimensional objects as such. It is far from clear how and whether these aspects of perception can be explained in the same computational terms as may conceivably be involved in the move from information about patterns of stimulation to information about the geometrical properties of whatever in the world is their cause (although even that, as Marr seems to admit, involves *a priori* assumptions on our part, even if they are not assumptions which we are conscious of making). It might, nevertheless, be thought a great advance in the psychology of perception if it were possible to provide an adequate theory of our ability to perceive three-dimensional objects as such.

Saying this brings me to my next point. It has been seen as a problem ever since Berkeley's *New Theory of Vision* how it is possible, given that the retina of the eye is a two-dimensional surface, for us to perceive a three-dimensional world. Berkeley, indeed, said explicitly, at the beginning of that work, 'It is, I think, agreed by all that Distance, of itself and immediately, cannot be seen.' Perception of distance is, he thought, possible only through the additional medium of touch. Since then a great deal of attention, by whole hosts of people, has been given to the various factors, including such things as stereopsis, which make distance perception possible. Gibson's emphasis on gradients of texture in the visual field is part of that general programme, although it has a particular importance in emphasizing the ground against which objects are normally seen and in undermining the tendency to think of the perception of objects as involving such objects stuck up in front of us without a context. Nevertheless, anyone who thinks, as both Gibson and Marr do, that it must be possible to explain perception of the world in terms of features of the visual system alone, has a problem. The fact that a three-dimensional array can project on to a two-dimensional surface does not of itself explain how we can see that array *as* three-dimensional.[14]

There is a sense in which this is not a problem for the Gibson of *The Senses Considered as Perceptual Systems* and afterwards, since he presumes that we are in a three-dimensional world and does not ask how our perception of that is related to the two-dimensional character of the retina. Indeed he thinks that irrelevant; *his* problem is, given that we are able to perceive the world via perceptual systems, what enables us to identify objects; and the answer lies in invariants. For Marr, however, who *is* concerned with how the system computes on the basis of information provided in retinal stimulation, it must be a problem how perception of three-dimensional objects is possible. Marr thinks that the solution lies in the idea of what he calls the '2½-D sketch' and its distinction from the '3-D model representation'.[15] Indeed, the perception by vision of objects involves, on his account, three steps, and three kinds of representation.

There is, first, what he calls the 'primal sketch', a representation of the 'two-dimensional image', which makes explicit intensity changes in it, and their location, geometrical distribution and organization. It corresponds directly to what happens at the level of the retina and is concerned with the information about what happens at that level. There will be, of course, many representations of this kind over time. From this is derived the 2½-D sketch, which is a representation which makes explicit details of surfaces from the viewer's point of view, their orientation and depth, and discontinuities in these which give rise to contour. The perception of objects in the world, however, is not merely a matter of how surfaces appear from the viewer's point of view; it is also a matter of the perception of objects with an identity and definite shape, and occupying a volume of space. The 3-D model representation is thus a representation of an arrangement of objects which is, as Marr puts it, object-centred rather than viewer-centred, as is the case with the 2½-D sketch.

The relation between the 2½-D sketch and the 3-D model representation has a certain similarity to that between Gibson's visual field and visual world, except that Gibson did not, in his first book, describe the visual field in terms of surfaces, and he in any case came to abandon the idea of the visual field later. But Gibson did not think in terms of a move from the one to the other. Marr does, so that the question how such a move is possible necessarily arises in his case. In effect, Marr claims that the system works with certain *a priori* assumptions about the general character of what can produce the details in the primal sketch, and computes the details of the 2½-D sketch within these 'constraints', as he calls them. Such constraints are in effect *a priori* hypotheses about the general character of what produces the pattern of retinal stimulation. Such 'constraints' must be built into the system; it is in effect already programmed to compute in this way.[16]

The 3-D model representation is tantamount to a schema of an object, which, as with Neisser's schemata, can make recognition of objects possible and so enhance further information pick-up. But the 3-D model representation must be initially related to and somehow derived from the 2½-D sketch. That is to say that there must be a relation between the schema or concept of an object that we have and the way or ways in which the organization of its surfaces appear to the viewer. Marr and Nishihara suggest that we construct the model representation (*the* schema) of an object by building it up on a modular or hierarchical basis from the component spatial organizations, so that each of these, as well as the whole, is seen in terms of some salient geometrical characteristic, particularly its natural axis, on which are likely to depend the variations in the organization of its surfaces as they may appear to the viewer. There is something a little odd in this account since it presumes that our conception of the shape and other spatial characteristics of an object is inevitably derived from how it appears to us visually. It is likely that our conception of objects in this way is based on all sorts of considerations, including in some cases convention.[17]

The whole three-stage account offered by Marr is necessary if recognition of objects, even if only in terms of their spatial and configurational properties, is to be possible. The representation of the object which is invoked in its recognition has to be derived from representations of how its configuration of surfaces appear to the viewer; and this in turn has to be derived from details of the primal sketch. This will be possible only if much is built in to make the computational derivations feasible. Are the terms of reference for all this acceptable? The following points are worth noting in this connection:

(1) The 2½-D representation is really a 3-D representation already if it is concerned with *surfaces*. Surfaces belong to three-dimensional objects. There is a difference between speaking of awareness of a two-dimensional array and speaking of the perception of surfaces. Berkeley was able to conflate these two because he thought of visual perception as consisting of an array of sensations in a two-dimensional field; this led in later writers to talk of, for example, a mosaic of sensations. But sensations do not by themselves provide information about the world, and there is no sense to the suggestion that perception itself could be of a field which is merely two-dimensional. Marr's use of the idea of a 2½-D representation is a partial recognition of that fact, but it introduces problems of its own.

(2) If we suppose that the brain works on a computational basis, then there has to be a move made possible by it from the pattern of stimulation on the retina to the cause of that, when that cause is construed in similar terms, that is, there has to be a move to something, whether or not 3-D, the causal role of which is confined to its planary aspects, so that it correlates directly with the 2-D pattern of excitation on the retina. There has to be a further move from this to the proper 3-D characterization of this cause, which provides *the* schema of the object or objects. Marr is therefore right in thinking that the whole process must involve three stages, *if* the total process is to be computational. But could computation make those moves possible?

(3) In so far as Marr is concerned with 'representations of' (where these amount to 'information about'), there are gaps (in effect those mentioned in my last paragraph) which have to be crossed: (a) the gap between the information provided in the primal sketch, which is merely information about a two-dimensional pattern of excitation, and the properly three-dimensional character of what is seen and which is the cause of this; (b) the gap between the latter construed merely as a set of two-dimensional surfaces as they are presented to the viewer and the objective facts about *the* three-dimensional character of objects. These gaps can be crossed only if the system is somehow built to cross them, that is, is already programmed to do so. But what does that mean in psychological terms, whatever it means in computational terms? It seems to amount to a series of moves from (i) what in terms of the system are the equivalent of sensations to (ii) appearances of the planary distribution of qualities belonging to whatever is responsible for the 'sensations', and from this to (iii) perception of objects which, because of their objective nature, are responsible for the appearances. Somehow, all this has to be put in terms of representations.

(4) It cannot be denied that Marr has done a remarkable job in showing that this is computationally possible *given the inbuilt 'constraints'*. But the existence of these constraints is crucial; all that Berkeley found puzzling is simply built into the system, and they would have been taken by Berkeley to involve the anathema

of innate ideas. If one waives any objection to these, Marr can be taken to have well identified the kinds of processes which must be realized in the nervous system, if it works computationally, in terms of a set of algorithms which make that possible. The point of departure in determining the realism or otherwise of it all must be the nature of the retinae of the eyes and of the processes which take place there. What happens after that has somehow to make possible perception of objects as objective, three-dimensional entities (plus, of course, a lot of other things which are not part of Marr's terms of reference).

A large question is whether the process in question is adequately put in terms of making possible a *representation* of objects. Is that the correct characterization of the output? What is it for the system to have a representation of three-dimensional objects except that that is how the final goal of the system is described? Given the way in which Marr defines 'representation' (as will be remembered from my earlier discussion of this), it will mean only that there is in the system a way of making explicit information about a three-dimensional world. This is derived, according to the theory, from what makes explicit information about much less than that. Apart from the difficulties, already noted, in that, is it the case that perceiving the world is simply a matter of such an organized system existing? The system will no doubt be necessary if such perception is to take place, but that is not to say that it is sufficient. If it is not, it may be that some different kinds of process, or perhaps additional ones, will have to be invoked in order to explain perception.[18]

What emerges from this once again is that an adequate account of what perception is becomes vital. I shall now turn in some detail to the question of what this must involve.

5

Perception II: What Is Perception?

INTRODUCTION

Marr has, at best, dealt with one, but only one, aspect of perception – spatial perception. I shall question later whether, as I have already indicated in effect, his sort of theory is adequate even for that. Perception is concept-dependent, and for spatial perception a concept of space and what is involved in that is necessary. For other aspects of perception other concepts are required. If one supposed that these other aspects of perception could be dealt with along the same lines as those used by Marr to explain spatial perception, it would surely be necessary to suppose that a vast number of other 'constraints' would have to be built into the system. Indeed, it would be plausible to maintain that one would be in the position taken by Fodor, of supposing that all concepts are innate, apart from those directly derivable by computation from concepts which are. Such concepts would have to be built into the system as 'constraints', in order to make any perception involving them possible. The only thing not innately determined would be what is given in sensation – the so-called representations of the primal sketch. Such a view, which of course goes well beyond anything that Marr contemplated, strains credulity, to say the least.

I have suggested that perception is concept-dependent, but I have not said what that means. There is also the question on what else perception is dependent. Is it, for example, sensation-dependent, belief-dependent, memory-dependent, and if so what is the relation of the various causal processes which are obviously involved to these considerations? If we go into these questions, it is likely that we shall become clearer about exactly what perception is; for we shall gain some insight into possible answers to the question 'X perceives something only if what?'. That is a clumsy question, but it is clear that, whatever one's views about the relation between meaning and truth-conditions, an inquiry into what conditions have to be satisfied if it is to be true that 'X perceives something' must cast light on the meaning of 'perceive' and thus help to provide some answer to the question 'What is perception?'. Whether one can give a list of the conditions the satisfaction of which is sufficient for the truth of 'X perceives something' is another matter. I shall try not to make too heavy weather of that point. Let us begin with sensation.

SENSATION

It was Thomas Reid in the eighteenth century who has been most insistent both on the distinction between sensation and perception and on the necessary dependence of perception on sensation.[1] It is desirable to emphasize both the distinction and the necessary dependence, because there has been a tendency in the history of thought to conflate sensation and perception in a way that distorts both concepts. It is that conflation that leads to the notion of sense-data or analogous notions, such as that of Hume's 'impressions'. Sense-data are supposed to be 'of' something; they have content and provide information about the world thereby. They are taken to constitute what is supposedly 'given' immediately to and by the senses. It is a question for epistemology whether there is any such thing, but that need not be our concern at present; for there is a place for the concept of sensation which is quite distinct from that, and this is something which Reid clearly saw.

Reid defined 'sensation' by saying (*Essays*, I. 1) that it 'is a name given by philosophers to an act of mind which may be distinguished from all others by this, that it hath no object distinct from the act itself'. There may be various things which one could object to in this, including the use of the word 'act'. Reid went on to say, however, that 'there is no difference between the sensation and the feeling of it'; that, with minor qualifications, seems evidently true of the most obvious candidate for the title of 'sensation' in ordinary parlance – pain. (The minor qualifications result from the fact that we might sometimes want to speak of a pain continuing when our attention is diverted from it and thus when, strictly speaking, we do not feel it. This connection with attention is important in itself and I shall return to it.)

Apart from pain, the occurrence of sensations of this kind is most evident in the case of other forms of bodily sensitivity, for example, in connection with touch. When we pass our hand over a textured surface we may receive certain sensations in our finger-tips, which will depend on the nature of the texture. To the extent that we are aware thereby of the texture of the surface, the less are we likely to be aware of the sensations as such. That is clearly a function of the 'direction' of our attention – whether our attention is concentrated on the surface of the object or on what is happening in our finger-tips. There may indeed be a certain vacillation of attention in this respect. I suggest that it is implausible to think that the sensations occur only when our attention is concentrated on them, as distinct from the surface of the object which produces them.

I have therefore argued elsewhere[2] that it is a reasonable thesis that the sensations occur even when our attention is not on them and we are not explicitly aware of them as such. Indeed the sensations in question affect the quality of the total experience which we are having when we feel the texture of the surface. They 'colour' it, so to speak, so giving the experience a totally different quality from that involved when we perceive the surface by some other means. A further point in this connection is the possible explanation, referred to in the second of the papers mentioned above, of the fact, which I am assured obtains, that panel-beaters usually put a cloth or tissue between their fingers and the panel, the smoothness of which they are trying to check. I suggest that they do this in order to obviate the possibility of their receiving distracting sensations in their finger-tips when they are anxious to concentrate all their attention on the surface of the panel. This also provokes questions about the role of a medium for a given form of perception.

It might be argued, and has been argued, that even if it is the case that one might justifiably speak of sensations of touch and suppose them to occur in some way when we use the sense of touch, this is no reason for thinking that sensations occur in the case of other senses, particularly vision. Gilbert Ryle, indeed, argued that there were no such things as visual sensations, except perhaps when our senses go wrong, as when we 'see stars'.[3] What makes touch different in this respect is that it is a contact sense, and in that way it is directly dependent on the effects that objects have on the body and on bodily sensitivity. By contrast, vision is a distance sense and has no necessary or even customary dependence on bodily sensations in the eyes. (Extremes of brilliance or intensity of light may produce such, as do analogous extremes in connection with hearing, but that does not affect the rule.)

All that is true, but it does not really affect the question whether there is a sensuous aspect to vision, involving something akin to what are evidently sensations in the case of touch. If there was nothing of that sort, there would be no special characteristic belonging to visual experience, other than what results from the fact that it is mediated by sense-organs of a particular kind, with a particular location and situation. But it is clear that visual experience does have a special quality of the kind in question, so that the analogy with touch, even if only partial, justifies our thinking in terms of visual sensation or sensations. (If one uses the plural here, it is evident that there are problems about how individual visual sensations are to be distinguished and identified, but no matter. In the history of thought on these matters the conflation of sensations with sense-data made the distinction between sensations derived from sight only too easy; but one should not be misled by this.)

That there is a sensuous aspect to perception, including visual perception, has also been argued recently by Christopher Peacocke, on a variety of grounds of varying persuasiveness.[4] Peacocke thinks, however, that such sensations are to be characterized in terms of an analogy between their qualities and those possessed by the objects of the corresponding perception. Thus the perception of a red object has a sensuous aspect which can be characterized only via an analogy with the quality of redness which the object possesses. For this reason he introduces the notion of 'primed predicates', such as 'red'' ('red prime'), which can be applied to the sensuous element or sensation which the corresponding perception involves. The perception of a red object involves a red' (red prime) sensation.

This seems to me a mistake. A burning sensation is not so called because of any feature of its cause, as a red' sensation is presumably so called because its cause is red. Burning does not necessarily produce burning sensations, and those which are so called are so because there is an analogy between their characteristics and the physical process of burning (which, of course, need have nothing to do with their origin). Hence, whatever sensations are brought about by the visual perception of something red may have no properties which can be characterized as amounting to redness or to anything which has an analogy with that. The way in which analogy enters into our characterization of sensations is quite different from that supposed by Peacocke.

For present purposes this is, perhaps, a minor point, although there are philosophical issues connected with it concerning the way in which terms like 'red' get a meaning for us, and what relation that meaning has to the sensations which occur when we see things as red. What is clear is that without those sensations someone could have at best only a partial understanding of what it is for things to be red; and if perception involves, as I believe it does, some such understanding, he could not perceive things as red in the way in which normal-sighted people do. Similar considerations apply, with modifications, to the perception of other properties of things, including their spatial properties.

It is worth noting that point because of the attention that has been given recently to the phenomenon of so-called 'blind sight'.[5] Weiskrantz discovered (and others have followed up the discovery) that some people suffering from certain forms of brain damage leading to apparent blindness over a part of the visual field can identify points of light in the part of the field of vision to which they are ostensibly blind at a level which is much better than chance. On the other hand, they have no consciousness of the points of light and do not believe that they are seeing them; they are simply, as they suppose, guessing. If the issue is put in that way, it might be suggested that these are cases of unconscious seeing, however that is to be explained. But the implication is that the lack of consciousness is due to the fact that there is no sensory or sensational aspect to the 'seeing'. Hence the term 'blind sight'.

There is a conceptual issue as to whether 'sight' is the right word to use in these circumstances, though psychologists might prefer to pay more attention, in effect, to the word 'blind'. The use of the word 'sight' presents an issue simply because some philosophers, as we shall see in more detail later, have tried to analyse 'sight', and 'perception' generally, entirely in terms of a specific form of causation of beliefs. It might be argued that the patients in question do not have beliefs about the points of light – they think they are guessing. But they might conceivably come to have such beliefs if they were convinced of the reliability of their supposed 'guesses'. If that were so, they would be caused to have such beliefs by, *inter alia*, the points of light. But the only reason for speaking of sight would be that the eyes were involved; they would be the means, causally, whereby the patients acquired the relevant information. It is not clear that this would be enough to justify speaking of 'sight', given that there were no visual experiences.

Moreover, it remains true that if someone were born without any visual experience whatever, he would never come to have any more than a partial understanding of what it is for things to have colour or brightness, or a whole host of other 'visual' properties of objects. Gibson, as I noted earlier, rejected any appeal, in a theory of perception, to cognitive processes. He also rejected an appeal to sensations.[6] But, certain kinds of information about objects is crucially dependent on the fact that it is mediated by processes involving sensation. For the possession of the requisite concepts in an adequate way depends on having visual experiences (and in some cases experiences connected with other senses). Moreover, although this is not a point which need be our immediate concern, someone who has no sensations cannot have any perception or appreciation of the aesthetic characteristics of things.

It must be noted that I have not said above that someone who lacks the relevant sensations can have no understanding whatever of the corresponding properties of things. The blind can have *some* conception of colour, particularly an understanding of the formal relationships between colours and, for example, any analogies which exist between colours and sensory properties the perception of which depends on the use of other senses, for example, the idea of warm and cold colours. Moreover, it might be possible for them to discriminate between colours in other ways than by sight, if, for example, any correlation exists between colour and some other detectable property. None of this belies the fact that they cannot have the understanding of colour that sighted people have, unless they have at some stage enjoyed the experience of sight. The same does not apply to spatial perception, since the perception of spatial properties and relationships is possible through other senses than sight, for example, touch. But, as is indicated by the reported experiences of those who have had their sight restored after congenital cataract, the spatial perception of the congenitally blind may well not be quite like that of sighted people.[7]

The relation between the sensations that a person may be having in perceiving things and how they look or otherwise appear to him is a complex one. There is, for example, the phenomenon of perceptual adaptation – the fact that sometimes when experience is distorted in some way things can come in course of time to 'look right'. It is reported, for example, that when subjects wear distorting spectacles or prisms, which invert or otherwise spatially distort the look of things by altering the pattern of excitation on the retina, things do after a time come to 'look right'.[8] It is never entirely clear what this means, but there is undoubtedly some sense in which this is so.

The same kind of thing occurs in the use of certain prosthetic devices, the immediate purpose of which is not to distort sense perception, but to supplement it when, for example, a specific sense is missing. There is a device entitled a 'tactile visual substitution system' (TVSS), whereby blind people are enabled to perceive what is in front of them by means of a television camera connected to a system of vibrating rods which stimulate the skin on their backs. After a time such people not only come to be able to detect by its means the spatial distribution of objects in front of them; they also report that they become less and less aware of the distribution of sensations on their back and more and more aware of how objects in front of them are distributed – to the extent that they feel inclined to speak of 'seeing' the objects or of their looking such to them.[9]

The sensations on their backs no doubt have what F. H. Bradley called 'volume' or 'voluminousness', in the sense that they are, as it were, spatially distributed over the skin; but they are not thereby distributed in the space in which the objects are eventually perceived as existing.[10] No doubt the subjects who underwent these experiences would never have had any spatial perception at all if they had no conception of space derived from the use of other senses. It remains true that the TVSS enabled them to have a form of spatial perception which they would not otherwise have had, that things came to appear to them in ways which would not otherwise have been available, and that this way of appearing was mediated by sensations which had voluminousness through their bodily location but which did not in themselves constitute a form of spatial perception.

It is arguable that one of the things which led Marr to the idea of the 2½-D sketch – the fact that random-dot stereograms devised by Bela Julesz, when viewed so that a pattern of randomly distributed dots is presented to one eye and a slightly shifted pattern is presented to the other, produce through retinal disparity an impression of one pattern or part of it floating in front of the other – is another example of the phenomenon of voluminousness and not, strictly speaking, an instance of spatial perception proper. Marr thinks otherwise and uses it as an example of how stereopsis can come about by computation from the details of the primal sketch. If I am right, however, the mechanisms involved in the reaction of the optical system to the retinal disparities produced by the random-dot stereograms might well afford sensory experiences which have voluminousness. Where a person already has the idea of depth, the sensory experience could manifest itself as an impression of depth; but that would depend on the existence of forms of spatial perception proper.

By itself, therefore, the so-called impression of depth which occurs in the case in question or in analogous cases is merely the having of sensations which have voluminousness. More is required for spatial perception proper than that, even when the spatial perception is restricted to surfaces. Voluminousness applies to sensations only, and it might be objected that the experience in the random-dot stereogram case does not consist merely of voluminous sensations but is an experience of volume. I have already noted, however, the effect on the situation that may be brought about by possession of a concept of space. It is worth noting in this connection the situation which holds good over after-images. In their case too, an experience consisting of sensations is naturally taken by the person concerned as an experience *of* certain things, for example, a pattern on the wall at which he is looking. Voluminousness in sensations can, when part of a perceptual experience, produce an experience of *as it were* spatial characteristics. But all that depends upon the possession of a concept of space.[11]

I have said enough to indicate at least some of the ways in which perception may rightly be said to be sensation-dependent. I must now turn in more detail to the part played in perception by concept possession and use.

CONCEPTS

I have already made reference to some of the ways in which concept possession determines what can be perceived and what cannot. That perception is concept-dependent in general is indicated by the fact that in order to perceive something we must perceive it as such and such. It is not of course the case that in order to perceive X I must perceive it as an *X*. The possibility of illusion and perceptual error in general rules out any such necessity. But I must perceive either it or something there as something. I put the matter in that slightly complicated way in order to take in the possibility of subliminal or unconscious perception. One can sometimes be said to have perceived something and there may be grounds for thinking that true without one's being in any way aware of that thing. But there could be no grounds for the making of that assertion if the context was not a perceptual one. Where, for example, grounds may turn up for thinking that I have seen someone in a crowd without being aware of having done so, it may well be right for someone to say that I did indeed see him without being aware of the fact. It could scarcely be right to say that I saw him *as* anything. But I must have been seeing *something* in a way that makes it appropriate to say that I saw it as something or other. If I was not seeing something as something or other I could not have been seeing anything.

So, all seeing involves seeing-as, all perceiving involves perceiving-as. The concept of seeing-as is a complex one. There are phenomena which fall under that concept which entail a fairly obvious use of the imagination, for example the seeing of a triangle as lying down or hanging from its apex, which Wittgenstein noted, among other things in his *Philosophical Investigations*, II, xi.[12] I shall discuss later whether there is a sense in which perception always involves imagination, but in the more obvious sense of 'imagination' which is applicable to the kind of example which I have just noted it is reasonably clear that perception does not always involve imagination, and *a fortiori* does not involve seeing-as or perceiving-as in that correlative sense. But in the more general sense, to perceive something as F is simply to perceive it as having a certain characteristic, and it is impossible to do that if one has no understanding of what it is for something to have a characteristic. But to have that understanding is to have the concept of F, and it is put to use in some way in perceiving whatever it is as F. To put the matter in a slightly different way – to have a concept of F is to know what it is for something to be F. To know what it is for something to be F involves knowing that an indeterminate list of things are so – things such as that being F involves being . . ., or that such and such a range of things are F. But it is important that that list is indeterminate. One cannot lay down a determinate set of knowings-that which are necessary and sufficient for knowing what it is for something to be F. To perceive something as F nevertheless entails having that knowledge.

Perception therefore presupposes knowledge. It might be thought that this presents a problem in that it is surely the case that knowledge itself depends on perception, so that if we accept all this we are involved in a circle. I shall return to this issue later, but it is worth noting now that the phrase 'depends on' does not necessarily imply that there is first perception and only then – later – knowledge. The two – perception of X and the knowledge of what it is for something to be X – might come together, but such that the one of them could not occur without the other. The same is true the other way round; when perception presupposes knowledge it does not necessarily do so in the sense that the knowledge has to precede the perception in time. It is simply that the perception of something as F cannot, logically, take place without the knowledge of what it is for something to be F. But they could both come together.

Apart from the kind of indeterminacy already described in what is involved in knowing what it is for something to be F, it must also be noted that knowledge of what it is for something to be F, whatever F is, need not be an all or none matter. How much one must know in order to know what it is for something to be F is not fixed and is a matter of degree. To perceive something as a cyclotron I must know something of what a cyclotron is, but I do not need precise knowledge of what it is. The same applies to every other concept, although the relative complexity of a concept delimits to some extent the range of things which are possible in this respect; the more complex the concept the more possibility of variation in what I have to know in order for it to be plausible that I have that concept. No concept is so simple, however, that one and only one thing has to be known in order to have it; there are no atomic concepts. (We shall see later that the conditions for the possibility of knowledge itself (that is, the conditions which must obtain if someone is to have knowledge at all) have implications for the preconditions for its being the case that one knows anything in particular.[13])

In order to be able to perceive something as F, however, it is not enough that one should have the knowledge of what it is for something to be F in some quite abstract sense. For that knowledge has to be applied to the object in a perceptual context; the concept has to be put to use in that context, and what that amounts to is a considerable problem. I tried to argue earlier that no one who had no visual experiences could have more than a very partial understanding of what it is for something to be red. The understanding or knowledge (and there is no relevant difference between these two in this context, since to know what it is for something to be F *is* to understand F-ness) that a congenitally blind person has of what it is for something to be red is a very abstract kind of knowledge, which is made less abstract only by whatever connections are available between it and perceptually based knowledge derived from other senses. The knowledge that a sighted and experienced person has of what it is for something to be red is not of that kind, as is indicated by the fact that he or she can identify red objects in a way that the blind person cannot. What is the relation between the abstract knowledge and the knowledge which is manifested in the perceptual identification of objects?

This is a problem which was seen by Kant in what he had to say in the section of his *Critique of Pure Reason* concerned with what he called the doctrine of the schematism of concepts. Kant was

most interested in the problem with respect to what he called
'categories' – formal and general concepts which are presupposed
in all judgements with respect to objective experience. The
problem is, as he admitted however, quite general. It is logically
possible, to use one of his examples, that someone might have a
formal understanding of what dogs are, in the sense that he could
give a formal definition of 'dog', without being able to recognize
any dogs when he saw them. What then makes perceptual recognition and identification of dogs possible for someone? Kant
himself claimed that it was the product of 'an art concealed in the
depths of the human soul' and was in some sense an aspect of the
imagination. It is clear that, if it is, this is not so in the sense in
which the examples of ways of seeing things which I noted earlier
in connection with Wittgenstein involve the use of the imagination. For they involve a very specific use of the imagination
which some might say involves reading things into the situation;
what we are concerned with now involves nothing of that kind
and is quite general.[14]

One particular phenomenon, however, which provides an
instance of what is involved in this in general, is the phenomenon
of things suddenly coming to look quite different because we
realize what they actually consist of, because we come to know
what we are seeing. This is an experience which more or less
everyone must have had. Someone who has had some relevant
experience of how things look (and what counts as relevant is a
complex question) may sometimes be able to work out for himself
what something he is told about must look like. It is conceivable,
for example, that someone who has the formal knowledge of
what a dog is, in Kant's example, but who has never seen a dog,
might be able to work out what dogs must look like in general.
But the phenomenon of things coming to look different because
of a realization that they are such and such requires no working
out on our part; it may be too sudden for that. A good deal of our
knowledge of things involves a general knowledge of how they
look because our knowledge of them has been gained through
experience. Conversely, but through the same connection,
knowledge can organize experience itself. That can be said to
involve the imagination, if only because these connections are
involved, though in a specific way, in the obvious and ordinary
uses of the imagination.

I have laboured these points because they are clearly relevant to the sense in which perception can be said to provide us with information about the world. Someone who, like Pylyshyn, maintains that the senses function as transducers to convert energy changes into coded information on which computation can work, or who, like Gibson, thinks of the senses as perceptual systems for abstracting information from the stimulus array, should be called on to explain how 'looks' figure in their account and how they explain the particular phenomena which I have noted. It might be said that for the purposes of cognitive psychology these phenomena do not matter. But they *do*, because a large part of our cognition of things is not independent of their looks. The role of the senses is not merely to furnish us with abstract beliefs, correct or incorrect, about the world. In our practical dealings with the world we need to know how things look, sound, smell, taste and feel. I shall consider in more detail the relation between perception and belief in the next section, but one more point needs to be noted here.

The concepts which we apply to experience in perception do not merely presuppose belief; they presuppose *knowledge*. To have the concept of X is to *know* what it is for something to be X, not merely to have relevant beliefs about what it is for something to be X. Whatever else human beings are, they are knowers, and could not have successful dealings with the world unless that was so. It might be objected, as in effect Socrates is made to do in Plato's *Meno*, that true beliefs are often good enough; a true belief about the location of something will get us to it just as well as knowledge of its location. Socrates is made by Plato, later in the same dialogue, to say that the trouble with true beliefs is that they are not constant or permanent enough in people's minds, and that is why knowledge is requisite in the end. Ultimately , it is only knowledge that is reliable in our dealings with the world. That may be so but it is not the only relevant point. It is also the case that someone cannot have beliefs unless he also has knowledge – not necessarily, of course, about the same thing, but about something relevant. One cannot believe that S is P unless one knows in some way what it is for something to be S and P. As I said earlier, that knowledge may be partial and is in any case a matter of degree, but it must exist to some extent and in some way. The implications of this point for our present concerns will emerge in due course. Meanwhile, I must give a little further consideration to the relation between perception and belief.

BELIEF

The view that it is the function of the senses to provide us with information is easily construed as the view that its function is to provide us with beliefs about the world (and, of course, knowledge too). Someone who sees that such and such is the case certainly thereby and *ipso facto* comes to believe that that is the case. If, however, he simply sees whatever it is as such and such he does not necessarily come to believe that it is like that. That fact is readily apparent in the case of some illusions. Someone who, being confronted with the Müller-Lyer illusion, sees the lines with arrowheads on them as of different length need not believe that that is how they are; he may indeed know that they are not. He may be inclined, tempted or disposed to believe that that is how they are, and if one asks 'Why?' the only possible answer is that it is because that is how the lines look to him.

In spite of this and similar considerations, some philosophers have wanted to analyse perception in terms of beliefs, although not always in a straightforward way.[15] The technical way of putting such a thesis is to say that perception is always epistemic. If what I have said about the Müller-Lyer illusion is right, then this is, on the face of it, a case of non-epistemic perception, although it may be that it can take place only if we have other, epistemic, forms of perception (for example, we can see the lines as of different length only if we see that they are set out opposite each other in a certain way, etc.). That is to say that non-epistemic perception is possible on the part of an individual only if he has epistemic perception, though not necessarily with reference to the same thing.

I make that last qualification because, in his first book, *Seeing and Knowing*,[16] which is in many ways a direct ancestor of his *Knowledge and the Flow of Information* referred to in a previous chapter, Fred Dretske argued that an analysis of epistemic perception, in terms of the truth-conditions for the assertion that someone perceives that p, necessarily involves reference to non-epistemic perception about the same thing. This is not the place to go into the details of the thesis, which is very much connected with the issue as to whether knowledge is to be explained in terms of justified true belief. (Chapter 3, in particular, is very explicitly concerned with that much discussed issue, contributions to which are so extensive as to constitute an industry.) Suffice it to say that, because to say that X sees that p implies that X knows or at least believes that p, one needs to make clear what makes it a case of *perceptual* knowledge or belief. Dretske thinks this is made clear if it is added that in order to perceive that b is P one needs to perceive b non-epistemically, and that non-epistemic seeing amounts simply to visual discrimination. This is a form of seeing which is not relative to the conceptual background or past experience of the perceiver, and makes it possible for seeing to take place *'without undermining the objectivity and publicity of what we see'* (p. 77, author's italics).

The problem about all this is that, whether or not we need such an absolute concept of non-epistemic seeing in order to explain why what is involved in epistemic seeing is in fact seeing, it is far from clear that visual discrimination answers to such a concept. Is visual discrimination a form of seeing which is not relative to any conceptual background? Visual discrimination is not simply reacting differentially to something within one's visual field, although it may presuppose something of that kind. To discriminate something visually is at least to see it as different from its background, and, in line with what I have already said about seeing-as, this must imply having a concept of difference.

This is a point of fundamental importance; it is a corollary of the point that all perception is concept-dependent. It is not part of that thesis that seeing something as different from its background implies seeing that it is different; but it *is* part of it that seeing something as different from its background implies knowing in some way and to some degree what it is for two things to be different. Let me emphasize once again that it does not follow from this that one has to know about difference *before* any seeing can take place; the seeing may bring with it the knowledge in question, and all that is entailed is that there cannot be seeing unless (logically) there is that knowledge.

The concept dependence of perception is quite general, and it applies to the spatial perception that Marr, for one, is so much concerned with. The fact that straightforward facts about the causal conditions of vision, such as the existence of retinal disparity, may lead to an impression of depth does not gainsay that claim. To override the claim, Marr would have to become involved in the kind of exercise that the Gestaltists engaged in, of seeking evidence to the effect that children with no concept of space whatever still have an impression of depth when there is retinal disparity in the stimulation of their eyes. That exercise was abortive in the case of the Gestaltists because one can never find children who are both young enough for it to be plausible that they have no concept of space whatever and old enough to act as suitable subjects.

T. G. R. Bower and others have claimed that there is evidence of shape and size constancy in infants a few weeks old, the evidence resting on what can be observed of their eye-movements following adults, such as mother, who attend to them.[17] But even such evidence does not quite meet the point, since what is observed is differential reactions, and to go beyond that to the claim that the infants have spatial perception involves an inference which requires some justification. The whole issue is clearly a matter of the relative contributions to perception made by knowledge and the satisfaction of causal conditions.

If I am right, what all this means is that whatever information is available in the stimulus array (to use Gibson's words) it will not be available *to the perceiver* unless he has the concepts necessary to make that possible. Nevertheless, the interaction between conceptual knowledge or understanding and the causal and other processes involved will not necessarily lead to belief about what is there, let alone knowledge. For, to see something as F is not necessarily to have any beliefs about it. Does it nevertheless lead to the receipt of information about what is there? Perhaps, but it would be otiose to insist on that unless there is evidence of the information being put to use. And that presupposes, amongst other things, concept possession and use. It is an extremely plausible thesis that the younger the child the greater will be the role played by causal processes. It is plausible if only because the building up of a conceptual structure is clearly a function of experience. If a child has at a very early age some understanding of spatial relationships it will be an understanding which is thin in comparison with what may hold good later. But such understanding is always a matter of degree. The relative contributions of different factors in perception is clearly an empirical matter. That perception is concept-dependent is not an empirical matter in the same way; it is a matter of what is involved in the concept of perception itself.

One final point before I go on to a further consideration. I have noted earlier the possible parts played in perception by imagin- ation, and in what senses of that term this is so. It would, of course, be foolish to ignore the part played as well by memory and the general effect of the past. Some cognitive psychologists tend to deal with this simply by writing into their informational flow-chart a box to indicate a function for information storage. But memory is a much more complex phenomenon than that. It is easier to make sense of what one perceives if it is familiar, or if that kind of thing is familiar, but what is involved in finding that thing familiar and finding that kind of thing familiar may be quite different. A further point is that one may find something familiar without any explicit recollection of when one experienced it or something like it before. A theory that connects memory essen- tially with information storage is of a part with a memory theory based on the idea of memory traces. That is to say that it presupposes the setting up and maintenance of some state of the system which has its effects upon other states of the system. But just as it is implausible to think of the belief that p in terms of the obtaining of one identifiable state, as we saw in chapter 3, so it is implausible to think of remembering that p in the same way. Yet it is clear that remembering that p in one way or another may affect in a variety of ways how one perceives the world. I shall not try to elaborate on this sort of point here, but it has to be noted.[18]

ATTENTION AND AGENCY

I made reference to one role of attention when speaking of the part that sensations play in perception, indicating that there may be a vacillation of attention in the case of touch between what is happening in our finger-tips and the texture or otherwise of the object touched. It is less clear to what extent such a phenomenon takes place in the case of senses such as vision which are not contact senses. In the case of sight our attention is normally on the object being perceived, and it takes an unusual degree of introspectiveness or some special quality in the experience itself for our attention to be drawn to that. It may well be the case that in large numbers of people it never happens; the qualities of the experience are not generally important to us and play no special role in our lives. But the fact that our attention is not normally drawn or directed to the experience is not a reason for saying that we are not attending to the object of perception either. Clearly we sometimes pay more attention to some things in our field of vision than to others; and what is in the centre of the field of vision, and is perceived with the greatest clarity because of the nature of our eyes, is normally attended to more than what falls at the periphery.

A good amount of psychological work has been done on the phenomenon of selective attention, when there is selection between alternative sets of information in the process of stimulation.[19] It is generally supposed that this is to be explained by appeal to selective mechanisms of some kind. It is conceivable that the same kind of thing might be at work when an oscillation takes place between the different 'aspects' or views of ambiguous figures. None of these theories, however, really gets to grips with what attention itself is. Attention is clearly an aspect of consciousness, whereby consciousness of something is enhanced by concentration on it. Unfortunately words like 'concentration' are near synonyms for 'attention' itself, so that what I have said could not be taken as an adequate definition of 'attention'. Yet most ordinary people would know what is being talked about when reference is made to the phenomenon.

Attention is not always selective. One can pay attention to everything that is before one, although, as a fact of human psychology, the span of attention, both temporal and spatial, is likely to be limited. Work has been done, indeed, ever since interest in the span of consciousness developed, mainly in the nineteenth century, on what those limits normally are. How much can one attend to at one time, and for how long? In trying to answer that question it is generally taken for granted that attention is something that can be intentional, even sometimes deliberate. On the other hand, we sometimes think of our attention being drawn to things. That, however, no more shows that attention is to be thought of as passive on occasion than the fact that we are sometimes made to do things by circumstances shows that the action in question is then to be construed as something passive. When our attention is drawn to things, our attention to them may be unintentional, but it is not non-intentional; it is not to be counted as falling outside the set of things which can be intentional (or unintentional). It follows that 'attention' is not entirely synonymous with 'consciousness'; for we can be conscious without our attention being directed to anything. Yet, when we are actually conscious *of something* it would not be unreasonable to claim that our attention is on whatever it is, at least to some extent or other. It is also likely that where attention to an object is involved in cases of perception there will be eye-movements of some kind which will not be totally involuntary.[20]

I put the matter in that rather indefinite way, because the issue is clearly an empirical one, or at all events it is so if the issue is whether active eye-movements are always involved in these cases. It seems clear, however, that without some active forms of attention on our part, and whatever makes that possible, the extent of our consciousness of the world would be extremely restricted. This is part of a more general issue concerning the extent to which perception depends on our being agents and thereby depends on activity on our part. Some psychologists have emphasized the extent to which perception depends upon activity on our part. Gibson is a notable example. For he thinks that the senses, considered as perceptual systems, seek or hunt for stimuli in order to pick up essential information in the stimulus array. Indeed, on this depends the successful detection of invariants in the changing pattern of stimulation over time.

In that sense, the pick-up of information about objects with an identity depends on our taking such action as will make that more probable. That, however, does not amount to a claim that information pick-up *necessarily* depends on agency on our part; it is merely that, as a matter of empirical fact, information pick-up will be less successful without activity on our part. In that sense, activity is something which is added on to the functioning of the senses as transducers, and facilitates that functioning so as to increase the possibilities of information pick-up. A purely passive creature which still possessed something playing the role which sense-organs have as transducers might still, on this account, have some perception of the world, but not so much and not so efficiently as an active human being.

The question is whether that is all that there is to it. How much would a creature really be able to perceive of the world if it was incapable of any active processes and could not be said to be an agent in any sense? It is arguable that the perception of the world as consisting of solid objects, and of objects occupying space generally, depends on our making active movements in relation to them;[21] and of course our perception of things with other properties depends on our perception of them as objects occupying space. Only in that case could objects be perceived as having surfaces and thereby having, for example, colours. (For the colours which solid objects have are normally surface colours, colours which extend over their surface and which do not necessarily permeate them as so-called film colours do in the case of, say, liquids.) If the perception of things as three-dimensional, in the sense of properly occupying space, depends on what we *do* in relation to them, this has obvious relevance to Marr's thesis about the acquisition of the so-called 3-D model or representation; for it will imply that however we are programmed and whatever computations go on, these will be insufficient if we do not *act* in relation to the world.

It is important to be clear what the issue is and what is at stake. There are some well-known experiments by Held and Hein,[22] which have often been taken to show the effects of active movement on the possibility of acquiring perceptual knowledge of the world. Kittens which were brought up without being allowed to more about, but which were nevertheless subjected to passive movement by being towed around a room in a cart, did not learn much about their environment, by comparison with kittens who were given free movement. There are perhaps many possible explanations of the facts, and it would be quite wrong to jump to the conclusion that the kittens saw nothing of their surroundings; still less that they were unable to see. (As has been put to me by Ulric Neisser, papooses surely see things in their surroundings!) What they failed to gain, certainly, was the sort of knowledge of their surroundings which can best be got through exploration. Presumably, in any case, they were not prevented from making any movement at all; they had to feed and could thus move parts of their bodies. It must be almost impossible to design an experiment which prevents any form of agency whatever, and one may have to have recourse to philosophical arguments which are relatively *a priori*.

Prima facie, there are many aspects of things such that it is difficult to think of our having any idea of them unless we can manipulate them in some way. Solidity, which, in the form of inpenetrability, Locke (in some views mistakenly) put into his list of primary qualities, is an instance of one of these. This is because the solidity of an object, its impenetrability to pressure or other forms of touch, is something which we could find out about only by means of something which is a kind of experiment on our part. It is not something which we could just see; nor would simple contact between the object and our body be enough.

But the causal notion of impenetrability and the notion of the identity of a body go closely together. For a body at a given time occupies a space which cannot then be occupied by other bodies, if they are solid. It may move to another space but only if that space is unoccupied, and this fact contributes to our understanding, and thus perception, of it as an object which has a certain identity. If objects could merge constantly with each other, as liquids may do, we should have no perception of them as preserving an identity over time. The identity of bodies is preserved when certain causal conditions are satisfied. Such causal conditions may vary to some extent with the kind of thing in question, but they must exist, as Kant saw in his 'Third Analogy' when he emphasized as a condition of the possibility of objective experience that there must in the objects of such experience be a reciprocity between one substance and another, so that there is a connection between the notion of identifiable substances and their causal relationships.

There is thus much more to objecthood than the possession of the merely geometrical properties of having three dimensions. Indeed, even the idea of the occupancy of space is not enough unless it is added that more than one object, or at any rate more than one solid object, cannot occupy the same space, because such objects are mutually impenetrable to the extent that this preserves identity. Thus Marr's attempt to show how it is possible to compute edges and boundaries in a way which leads to the setting up of the 3-D model representation is not nearly enough to show what makes perception of *objects* as such possible, if those objects are the sort of thing which occupy a physical world.

Without that last qualification, it might be thought that there could still be perception of three-dimensional volumes having properties such as colour which might distinguish them. But what, given change over time, could, in that case, give sense to the idea of an object retaining an identity over that time? It might be suggested that if, as a matter of contingent fact, one volume retained the same colour throughout, while everything else around it changed, this would be enough for us to see it as the same thing throughout. But this would be so only because it would give the impression, because of its lack of change, that it was unaffected by its circumstances; we should then be, as it were, reading into it something about the causal conditions for its persistence, and we could not do that unless we knew something already about causal conditions and their connection with identity.[23] Could this be something which we could do without having learned to do so?

There is a connection between this kind of thing and the notion of conservation with which Piaget has had much concern. Indeed, Jerome Bruner has said, 'Perhaps the psychology of conservation, indeed, all forms of invariance, involve the recognition that the same thing can take many guises and still be the same thing.'[24] One might add that it is not merely a matter of the recognition that the same thing can do this; the perception that it actually does so depends on the recognition that both its identity and the variation of its guises depend on its satisfaction of certain causal conditions of which we must have some prior understanding. When a child learns that something, a quantity of liquid, say, or a lump of plasticine can take different shapes and still remain the same thing, he or she is learning not merely what one might call the principle of identity in difference (as is implied in Bruner's formulation) but some of the principles of *physical* identity. This is a matter of the causal principles which sustain its identity as the kind of physical thing it is, and which allow its transformation in certain ways but not others.

Piaget's conservation studies are essentially studies of children's ability or inability at different ages to recognize something as maintaining its identity as a substance, or in respect of some important property of a substance, such as mass, despite apparent transformations brought about causally in it. But the very ability to perceive something as a physical object presupposes *some* form of understanding of that kind. One cannot perceive the physical world which we occupy in any adequate way without a general understanding of this kind. Some degree of conceptual understanding of the world is thus a precondition of the possibility of perception of it. This is of course yet another example of the principle that all perception is concept-dependent, but it is a particularly fundamental one.

But the crucial point, as far as concerns the issues being raised in this section, is that we could have no understanding at all of the causal principles which go with the principles of identity for physical things, if we had no experience of ourselves interacting causally with things though our own bodies while retaining a sense of our own identity throughout. This is a central point in Kant's so -called 'transcendental deduction' – that a condition of the possibility of our having objective experience of the world is that, as he puts it, 'it must be possible for the "I think" to accompany all my representations' (*Critique of Pure Reason*, B131). That is to say that in perceiving the objective world it must be at least possible for me to be conscious of the experiences I am having as *my* experiences and thus the experiences of a single self. The objective counterpart of this is that the objects of those experiences must themselves be seen both as having an identity over time and being subject to causal principles. But – although Kant does not say so, this point being in effect left to Schopenhauer – all this depends on the active interaction between ourselves and the world of physical objects that our body makes possible. Part of the discovery of what bodies are and are capable of is the discovery of what our own bodies are and are capable of. We find out about solidity, for example, through the discovery of what kinds of resistance bodies make to our own bodies. This presupposes not only a physical interaction between ourselves and other objects, but an activity on our part to make that interaction possible.

To insist on this is not to think of a child, in initiating this understanding, as engaging in an experiment with regard to nature. An experiment, if it is to be a genuine one, presupposes a question put to nature, and the child is not capable of formulating any such question, unless it already has some conception of the world, against which the question might be put. I am saying only that an understanding of what is involved in a physical world depends on and presupposes interaction between ourselves and it; and such interaction is not one that takes place simply between our body and other bodies considered on a par, it involves bodily action on our part in a way that implies agency. And this in turn implies a sense of our own identity, against which what is identical and what is not in the world around us can be determined.[25]

A further caveat that must be made is that I am not saying that all perception must *ipso facto* involve our doing something. Individual cases of perception may or may not involve that, and, as I suggested earlier, the successful determination through perception of what is before us may well involve action on our part, as Gibson, for one, has insisted. My point here, however, is the quite general one that a perceiver must be an agent too; otherwise there would be no possibility of the would-be perceiver attaining the conceptual understanding necessary for perception of a physical world. And without that he would not be a perceiver in any sense that matters.

I said earlier that Marr's attempt to show how it is possible for a system to compute edges and boundaries in such a way as to enable the setting up of the 3-D model representation is not enough to show what makes perception of physical objects possible. Even Marr's account of what happens is subject to the existence of inbuilt constraints, which amount to *a priori* concepts of space in Kantian fashion. What I am now saying is that such an *a priori* concept of space must remain merely formal unless some additional account is offered of how such formal concepts are given embodiment in experience. That implies once again something like the Kantian doctrine of the schematism – a story about how the purely formal understanding is encashed in experiential terms. My claim here has been that if the formal understanding of space and its occupancy is to become an understanding of a physical world there is required bodily action on our part.

To put the matter in that way might, however, suggest that the formal understanding is innate, and that this is then given application in experience if the proper conditions are satisfied. That is *not* what I am suggesting as likely; rather, the understanding, even if an inchoate one, of what it is for there to be physical objects occupying space is likely to emerge in the course of our perception of the relationship of things in the world to our bodily action. It is this last thing in particular which makes it insufficient to offer a theory which regards perception as the result solely of interaction between processes of stimulation and concepts or principles of organization, whether inbuilt or acquired. It is impossible to ignore the part played by agency in the total picture, however large or small a part it plays in particular instances of perception. (And once given the satisfaction of the general condition about agency, to the effect that a perceiver, that is, one who *can* perceive, must be an agent too, the part played by our active agency in individual cases of perception must be extremely variable.)

CONCLUSION

I put as part of the title of the previous chapter the question 'A proper view of input?' It ought to be apparent by now that any theory which thinks of perception simply in terms of the transduction of energy input into coded information must be considered insufficient, whether or not it is supposed that the programming principles for the decoding of the information are inbuilt or not. Perception is a much more complicated matter than that, and many other factors are involved, such as sensation, imagination, attention and agency.

Perception is of course *of* things, and in that sense involves intentionality. Someone who thinks that the function of perception is to set up a representation of things has to explain how it is possible for such a thing to be *of* the things it is supposed to represent – how, as it is sometimes put, relying on an analogy with language, such representations can have a semantics and not merely a structure or syntax. Fodor, for one, clearly thinks this the great and most important question for the philosophy of mind, but can only gesture in the direction of an answer. Dennett, by contrast, thinks that there is no answer if the question is posed in realist terms, and thinks that the only course of action is to take an instrumentalist attitude to it, suggesting that taking a so-called intentionalist stance to people may be useful for the purpose of predicting their behaviour, but no more .

My reference to the part played by attention in perception is clearly a reference to one important manifestation of intentionality, since, as I indicated in the last section, to attend to something is to bring it about that one is conscious of it. It might be argued that if all consciousness were like that involved in having sensations one would not need to be over-concerned with it; but it is not, and even if perception involves sensations, one's consciousness in perceiving is not normally directed to *them*. On the other hand, there are manifest causal processes which take place in perception. Our sense-organs are stimulated and this leads to complex neural processes as a consequence. The virtue of the information-processing model is that it provides an intelligible construal of those causal processes, even if the details of them require for their setting out all the ingenuity of a Marr. The details of the third level of explanation, as expounded by Marr – the account of how the information processing is realized in physical terms – can then be handed over to the physiologist.

Such an account has nothing to say about sensations, however. Those philosophers who have embraced functionalism as the most satisfactory theory of the mind–body relation have sometimes seen difficulties in how sensations are to be brought within such an account.[26] Some, for example Sydney Shoemaker, have thought that one can deal with sensations simply by asserting their identity on a token–token basis with certain brain processes. It is very doubtful if such a move does justice to the facts about how sensations 'colour' our perceptual experience.

When one turns to the other factors that I have sought to show as involved in perception, such moves go nowhere. The consequence of this is that the relation between perception as a whole and the recognizable causal processes which are undoubtedly involved becomes most obscure. The same must hold good of the beliefs which perception often, if not always, gives rise to. I set out in an earlier chapter the problems inherent in the question just what is involved in someone's having the belief that p. Even if having the belief that p is in some sense a state of the person concerned it is not a state which is plausibly to be identified with any single physiological state of a person or his brain, unless the state is to be specified simply as whatever state has such and such a place within the person's belief system so that he perceives things in such and such a way and acts in this or that way accordingly. None of that, however, is likely to give much encouragement to anyone who is looking for a clear-cut, physically based, account of human psychology.

Unfortunately, I fear that that is how it is, and the lesson to be learned from my inquiry into the presuppositions of perception is that we are not at all near to understanding how perceptual processes are realized in physical and physiological terms. We may understand some of it, but we do not understand it as a whole – not nearly. It is of no avail to try to avoid such a conclusion by saying that the trouble lies in the espousal of folk psychology and the very acceptance of such folk-psychological concepts as perception, for the reasons which I set out towards the beginning of this book. If we say that there just *is* input to the human physiological or physical system, that there are processes within that system which are affected by it, and there is consequent physiological or physical output, we are left with a situation of such complexity that we can hardly begin to deal with it. Human beings do perceive, they do act, and they do much that intervenes between those two. We understand much of that in folk-psychological terms, and psychologists have added much to that understanding. But we cannot short-circuit what has to be done to connect that with the details of the physical and physiological system. We are miles (if that is not a grossly understated use of a metaphor) from a complete understanding of that, and should be thankful that we know and understand the little that we do.

That having been said, and the sermon having been brought to an end for the time being, there are further complications to be surveyed, arising out of genetic or developmental issues, and I shall turn to those in the next chapter. Meanwhile, let me emphasize again that perception is certainly subject to causal processes, some of which are fairly obvious, others of which can be sorted out only after detailed empirical inquiry. Moreover, there will be occasions when the nature of the perception will be explained simply by reference to them, for example perhaps in the case of sensory illusions. At other times, however, the explanation may well be much more complicated. There is no single rule.

6

The Effect of the Past

LEARNING, EXPERIENCE AND KNOWLEDGE

To think of human beings in information-processing terms is to try to explain what is in that case seen as output by reference to the input, together with whatever central processes need to be invoked to mediate between the two. There is a consequent tendency to think that an explanation of the output in these terms must invoke processes which are more or less contemporaneous with it. The past enters the picture only via its effects on what is present, depending on the way in which central processes are thereby modified. I indicated briefly in the previous chapter that this tends to be seen in terms of storage processes; information is stored in such a way as to affect subsequent input, with consequent effects on output. I suggested in that context that memory was in fact a much more complicated phenomenon than that.

In any case, however, it does not seem to be the case that the past always affects how we perceive something by way of something that we remember of the past. We may, for example, have learned to see something in some way, so that this way in which we now see it is clearly affected by the past, through that learning; but we may remember nothing of that learning process. Learning is not straightforwardly a memory phenomenon or process, although it is clearly a way in which the past may affect the present. To suppose, therefore, that one can deal with the effect of the past by reference to some process the function of which is the storage of information is not only an over-simple construal of memory, it is also an over-simple model for an understanding of the effect of the past on present cognitive processes, quite generally.

It might be objected that the effect of learning is surely to modify the state of the organism in such a way that it both perceives things and does things differently as a result. Why therefore cannot we be content with the attempt to explain how it perceives and what it does by reference to contemporary input and contemporary central states? According to one, prevalent, version of folk psychology those central states will consist of complexes of beliefs and desires; input interacts with those states and modified behaviour occurs accordingly, provided, of course, that input is sufficiently relevant to the central states to make genuine interaction possible. There is a sense in which, at its most general, this framework of explanatory ideas has elements of the truth. In learning there must be an interaction between experience and prior understanding. Although this inevitably raises the problem how learning can ever get off the ground – a problem to which I shall return shortly – the general conception of learning is not in dispute. The question is rather how that general conception is to be given detail. In what precise way is experience assimilated, so as to change the cognitive state of the person in such a way that, given relevant motivational factors, that person will behave in new ways when reacting to the perceived environment?

My use of the word 'assimilate' will suggest to some readers the views of Jean Piaget. In his view, the cognitive development of an organism is in large part a matter of its assimilating features of the environment and of its accommodating itself to that environment, in such a way as to produce a state of balance or homeostasis in its relationship to the environment. In fact, an appeal to homeostasis does not by itself make clear how any general principles of development are to be understood in its terms. Piaget spent a good deal of his life trying to light upon other principles akin to that of homeostasis which would explain development as such. He invoked principles such as that of homeorhesis which he derived from the work of the biologist C. H. Waddington and, towards the end of his life, that of phenocopy, derived from the work of evolutionary biologists seeking a compromise between Darwinism and Lamarckianism. These issues need not be our concern at present.

It is perhaps natural, all the same, for a biologist to think in some such way, and Piaget's attempts to express the principles underlying so-called cognitive development in biological terms were persistent, even unrelenting. But to speak of a person assimilating the experience to which he is subject is, as it stands, just a metaphor. All that it can really be taken to mean in any literal sense is that the course of experience makes a difference to how he sees the world and how he is inclined to behave in accordance with that perception. That is to say no more than that he has so learned to see the world and has so learned to behave. There is no point in leaping to a biological model in order to interpret that.

Once again, although human beings are undoubtedly biological entities, the exact relation between what we know of their biology and what we know of their cognitive processes and of the development and modifications of these through learning is undoubtedly a very complex matter. The understanding of that relation is not helped by resort to the information-processing model; for one of the crucial questions at issue is whether learning processes can adequately be explained in computational terms. To suppose that they can be is to suppose that the end-product of a learning process is arrived at through the application of computational principles to material which is already there in some sense, however much this is modified by interaction with input from transducers. If the issue is put in the terms of the representational theory of the mind, new representations are all products of the application of computational principles to already existent representations, and in that sense they are not fundamentally new. The so-called new structures are merely reorganizations and recombinations of existing structures, and the function of input processes is in effect to trigger off such restructurings.

This conception of things has some similarity to what is involved in the theory of recollection which Plato puts forward in his dialogue, the *Meno*. For that theory too is put forward as a theory of learning, in response to a dilemma, labelled by Socrates 'sophistical', but treated by him and Plato seriously all the same. The dilemma which starts from the superficially attractive principle that we either know something or we do not leads to the conclusion, by each of its horns, that learning is impossible. For if we know the thing in question already there can be no question of our learning it, whereas if we do not know it at all, if it is not even before the mind, we will not recognize it when we come to it, so that there is no 'it' for us to learn.

In order to dispel the paradox one needs at least the recognition that knowing something is not an all or none matter, and this entails a better conception of knowledge than the one presupposed by the dilemma. Plato does not apparently recognize this in the *Meno*, although it is arguable that he may have had some insight into the issue by the time he came to write the *Theaetetus*, where the dilemma is reinvoked to show that it leads to another conclusion – the impossibility of false belief. Instead, in the *Meno* he says that learning is in fact recollection; in what we ordinarily call 'learning' we are really being reminded of things which we once knew and now know only implicitly at best; hence, what is in fact implicit knowledge is made explicit in this way. Experience merely reminds us of this previous knowledge, in effect triggering off the recollection.

In the *Meno* Plato says that the soul has come to the knowledge so triggered off in previous lives, but since the acquisition of that knowledge must itself have involved recollection according to the theory, this view generates an infinite regress. There is no indication in the *Meno* that Plato was aware of that fact, but when he reinvokes the doctrine of recollection in the *Phaedo* (which he does with a more or less explicit reference to the discussion of the *Meno*) he contents himself with the claim that we are equipped with certain sorts of knowledge at birth. There is therefore innate knowledge.

Until recently most commentators have thought this claim absurd, although innate ideas and innate knowledge were appealed to by the rationalist philosophers of the seventeenth and eighteenth centuries. Chomsky's revival of 'Cartesian linguistics' and his claim that the basic or deep structure of language must be something that we are born with has, however, given new life to these ideas. The epistemological basis of Chomsky's claim is the thought that there is no way in which a child can derive the grammar of a language from the 'corrupt' data which are available to him from what adults say in his presence.[1] But this supposed epistemological basis for the theory has been seen by many as fitting in with the ways in which it is natural to think of individuals when they are construed either in biological or in information-processing terms. For the input, it is thought, can be used by the organism only if there is something inbuilt into it which makes that possible.

In what I have just said I have in effect distinguished between epistemological considerations which are supposed to lead to a doctrine of innate knowledge and other theoretical considerations. This is a point of some importance. There is nothing in these other theoretical considerations which necessarily suggests that it is *knowledge* that is inbuilt or innate. Both the biological and the information-processing models suggest only that certain kinds of *structure* are inbuilt in order that input can be utilized by the system. Chomsky did, originally, sometimes speak of 'knowledge' in presenting his theory, and what he said about the child's position in respect of the data available to him makes the child sound like an empirical inquirer, a little scientist, trying to make sense of the available evidence by inference to the best explanation. Subsequently, however, he has tried to play down the claim that he is arguing for innate *knowledge*, or has claimed that such knowledge is tacit only, as is also the knowledge involved in knowing a particular language.

Unfortunately, it is not altogether clear what is to be made of the concept of tacit knowledge. The term 'tacit knowledge' was introduced by Michael Polanyi in order to categorize all those cases in which people seem to know things without being able to spell out or make explicit what they know.[2] It has been taken over and used in a more circumscribed way by several people working in the general area of cognitive science in order to deal with those cases where it seems explanatorily useful to appeal to knowledge without it being implied that the person in question can spell out the content of the knowledge in question.[3] Put in that way, the appeal to the notion seems to have an instrumentalist bias. I noted in chapter 3 Dennett's use of the idea of tacit representation, according to which a tacit representation occurs when the system involved is simply an analogue of one in which certain information is explicitly represented. Dennett's approach is explicitly instrumentalist. Pylyshyn (p. 245) maintains that the notion of tacit knowledge is 'a generalization and extension of the everyday notion of knowledge (much as the physicists' concept of energy is an extension of the everyday notion)'. That is all very well, but one needs to know the basis of the extension and how much of the everyday concept is retained in that extension.

As I said earlier, this is a matter of some importance. For in order to attribute knowledge, in the everyday sense, to something certain things have to be presupposed. There is much argument in the philosophical literature as to whether the concept of knowledge is to be analysed adequately, as it was traditionally thought that it could be, as justified true belief. Whatever is the correct view on that, it is generally held that knowledge normally involves at least belief on the part of the knower, truth on the part of what is known, and some reliable connection between the two. But since belief is the attitude appropriate to the truth, it is difficult to see how one could attribute belief, and *a fortiori* knowledge, to something if it had no conception of what truth is. I have argued elsewhere[4] that it is impossible to see how a concept of truth could be acquired except in a social context. If all this is right, the idea of innate knowledge is ruled out.

Does the same apply to tacit knowledge? Unless that concept is crucially different from that of knowledge *simpliciter*, the answer must be 'yes'. But if it is so crucially different it can be called 'knowledge' only in an 'as if' sense; that is to say that all that we are saying by its use is that the behaviour to be explained is the sort of thing which we would explain by reference to knowledge if only . . . If only what? Presumably, if only that to which the tacit knowledge is attributed satisfied the conditions for the attribution of knowledge proper. If that is the case I take it that tacit knowledge is not knowledge at all, properly speaking. If someone denies this, it is incumbent upon him to explain why the term 'knowledge' is being used and in what sense.

The notion is not, as Pylyshyn claims, simply a scientific extension of the common-sense concept, since it has not been defined in such a way that the basis of the analogy with the common-sense concept is made clear. The concept, as explained by Polanyi in terms of the tacit knower not being able to spell out or make explicit what he knows, presupposes for its application the satisfaction of the conditions for the applicability of the common-sense concept; for it is not an extension of that concept, it *is* that concept restricted to cases in which the knower cannot make explicit what he knows. It is certainly the case that the only grounds for speaking of tacit knowledge in connection with what people are born with is that *if they had knowledge at all* it would have to be tacit in this general sense. But does it make sense to say that they have knowledge at all if the condition about having a conception of truth, or at any rate a conception in some possibly minimal way of what it is to be right and wrong, cannot be satisfied? And surely it cannot be.

This is not to say that much is not inbuilt into any individual who is capable of learning through experience. There are good reasons for rejecting the purely empiricist conception of learning which makes it entirely a matter of how experience 'falls' and makes the individual who learns totally plastic in this respect.[5] Experience has to be used, so to speak, and it is what is built into the organism that makes that possible. But what is so inbuilt cannot be knowledge. Once again the underlying problem is to relate these, presumably biological, facts about what individuals are born with to a story about the growth of knowledge as the result of experience. The relation remains obscure, although it is fairly clear that what people are so born with makes possible various innate dispositions and capacities. A capacity, however, does not necessarily amount to knowledge; fish can swim and have the capacity to do so, but it cannot be said that they know how to do so.

Fodor has argued that there must be innate concepts and indeed that all concepts must be either innate or derivable from innate concepts by computational procedures.[6] Part of his argument rests upon the consideration that the only conceivable way of understanding concept acquisition is in terms of what Peirce called 'abduction', or in terms of the idea that in constructing a concept we are constructing something like a theory, in terms of which the facts are to be explained. Theories of this kind need to be prior to the observations which are to be interpreted in their terms. If concept acquisition is conceived in this way there must be concepts prior to any experience, and so-called concept acquisition is either the fitting of these concepts to experience or the formation of concepts out of those which already exist by some constructive process. Strictly speaking there can be no really new concepts. Fodor insists that there is no other way in which to understand the formation of concepts and that if this is so there is no way of escaping his conclusions.

We are thus presented with a dilemma, which is not unrelated to that of the *Meno*.[7] Any concept, even a technical one such as that of a quasar or transistor, must either be innate or derived from concepts which are innate by a constructive process such as that involved in computation. In the *Meno* Plato tries to seek corroboration of his theory by an appeal to a mathematical example; he purports to show that a slave-boy already knows the solution to a mathematical problem (about the length of the side a of a square twice the area of a given square) and has only to be reminded of what he knows by being asked certain questions. In point of fact the questions which Socrates asks are no doubt leading questions, and many have seen in what Socrates does a good example of teaching, in spite of Socrates' denials of that. But the example of 'learning' in question is one where the knowledge acquired is *a priori*; it is not implausible to assert, in connection with at any rate *some* cases of *a priori* knowledge, that the new knowledge arises from a sorting out, and a working out, of the implications of what is already known. These processes may be extremely complex, and one should not take what I have said as suggesting that mathematics, for example, is thereby shown to be trivial. Far from it. All the same, it is not by any means the case that all learning is like the working out of a mathematical solution. Nor are all concepts simply reconstructions of old ones.

The reason for this is that the interrelations between conceptual understanding and experience are more complex than Fodor supposes to be the case; and this means in turn that concept acquisition cannot always be construed as simply involving abduction (or, as it has sometimes been put, inference to the best explanation). One might say that the picture of the infant's relation to the world which Fodor draws is once again very much that of the child as a young scientist. Apart from all else, such a view underplays the extent to which the processes involved in experience are simply causal, the extent to which experience just causes us to see things in certain ways.

Aristotle asserted at the beginning of his *Posterior Analytics* that all learning depends on prior knowledge. I believe that this is a profound remark, but there are certain things to note in relation to it. First, the claim that all learning depends on prior knowledge does not entail that all new knowledge is some kind of transposition of old knowledge. Second, it does not imply that all acquisition of knowledge is the result of learning. Experience can make us see that certain things are so. We may not be able to see them in that way unless we have the concepts which are presupposed in so seeing them. That fact, however, does not go against the idea that we may be *caused* to see them in that way. The same applies to the conceptual understanding itself; experience may bring it about causally that we have a certain conceptual understanding. Once again, it may well be the case that this will not happen if we do not already have certain other forms of conceptual understanding; but it does not follow that the new understanding is a mere rearrangement of what exists already. Given some prior understanding, experience can cause us to see things as we have not done in the past.

Nevertheless, some account is called for as to how this starts in the first place. Otherwise, we must inevitably have recourse to the idea of innate knowledge. Andrew Woodfield, who undoubtedly has a due sense of the problems here, has suggested that concepts come into being out of what he calls 'protoconcepts', and these are in some way tied to what he calls 'recognition-schemas'.[8] Protoconcepts lack certain properties which he rightly thinks concepts must have. Concepts are, he says, 'network-dependent'; that is to say that they have of necessity interconnections, so that they form an 'inferentially integrated network', and cannot stand on their own. In that respect they are like beliefs, which, as I suggested in the previous chapter, cannot be construed in an atomistic way; and that similarity is not surprising, since concepts and beliefs both involve knowledge. Belief, indeed, itself presupposes concept possession.[9]

Protoconcepts, Woodfield claims, *can*, by contrast, stand on their own. Secondly, they do not need to constitute contents of the mind which are conceptually similar to that of other people; they are not, that is to say, socialized. Recognition-schemas, by contrast, are 'formed by a process of adaptation to the objective groupings that are found in S's environment' (where S is the child in question). That is to say that they arise via a process which constitutes epigenesis. But Woodfield insists that they have to be representational as well; or, to put the matter in other terms, they have to have content.

There are very considerable problems in all this. The last point mentioned – that of the link between epigenesis and content – raises the question how a merely biological process of adaptation can come to have as its result anything which can justly be called 'recognition', since that seems to imply something like knowledge. What is said about protoconcepts, on the other hand, seems

to imply only that before the stage at which full concept possession can be ascribed to a child *some* 'cognitive state' must be
ascribable to it, if only because otherwise it would not be possible
to categorize its processes of adaptation to the environment as
involving *recognition*. Hence, what Woodfield has to say reveals,
as I have said, a just appreciation of the problems, but on his own
admission it is scarcely more than that.

KNOWLEDGE AND ITS CONDITIONS

I have maintained, earlier in my discussion, that to have the
concept of X is to know what it is for something to be X, and I
have pointed out that this normally involves more than the purely
formal understanding that may be involved in the ability to
provide a definition of X; it also involves some ability to pick out
instances of X. To say this is (a) to emphasize the fact that having
a concept entails having knowledge (and the knowledge that is
involved in understanding in particular), and (b) to emphasize the
extent to which the having of a concept implies an ability to
recognize cases, and thus also implies something like what Woodfield has in mind in speaking of recognition-schemas. I agree with
Woodfield also in insisting on the fact that conceptual understanding necessarily has a social dimension, as does knowledge
generally. Finally, I agree with him about the desirability of
having something to say about the 'cognitive state' of a child
before full-blown conceptual understanding has emerged. For
reasons which I shall set out directly, I also think it is desirable to
avoid appeal to innate concepts.

At least some of the problems implicit in all this will be
obviated by the recognition of certain points about the concept of
knowledge. In the first place, as I said in chapter 4, knowledge is
a matter of degree; it is not an all or none matter. Hence, the fact
that a child at a certain stage of his or her development does not
have a full-blown concept of X is not in itself a reason for denying
him or her any knowledge whatever of the matter. The ability to
see something as X, which is presupposed in Woodfield's claim
that recognition-schemas have to be representational, itself presupposes having some knowledge of what it is for something to be
X. But that knowledge can be as minimal as one likes, and need

have little in the way of connection with other knowledge. That is not to say that it involves nothing of that kind (for to admit that would be to allow atomistic concepts); it is to say that its ramifications can be both slight and inexplicit. Because all this is a matter of degree, it follows that no answer can be given to the question when the child acquires the first concept; there is indeed *no* first concept in any real sense.

On the other hand, whatever understanding does exist must be linked to such differential reactions to features of the environment as are possible for the child. But such differential reactions involve also differences within *experience*, since a child is not just a biological organism, but a person capable of experiencing the environment, in a way which something without a mind would be incapable of. That is to say that a complete account of these matters would have to recognize the part played by *perception*, not merely differential reaction or even adaptation. The child must be born with the potentiality for all this; but that is not to say that it is born with innate recognitional and conceptual capacities, merely the capacities for acquiring these.

In the case of animals which, as the ethologists make clear, react differentially to certain features of their environment as a matter of instinct, one may be in doubt as to whether it is really appropriate to speak of them as perceiving these features as such and such. One cannot be quite definite about the matter, because there might be other grounds for attributing to them 'seeing-as' in general; if there were such grounds, there could not be an objection to saying that it is possible that they see something in one way rather than another, although they have not learned to do exactly that. Given a background potentiality for seeing-as, there might possibly be a causal explanation of the fact that they see some particular thing in a particular way.

Some geese react with alarm to a certain patterned object when it is towed in one direction over them, but do not react when it is towed in the opposite direction. They do so, we might possibly say, because they see it in the one case as a hawk and in the other as a goose. The question is whether we should really be justified in so speaking. If they have not learned to see things in this way, then unless it is appropriate to speak of their seeing things as such and suches in general (and that possibility presupposes the satisfaction of all the conditions of seeing-as, including concept possession), we should have to speak of them merely as exhibiting differential reactions to stimulus patterns. On the other hand, if it *is* appropriate to speak of their seeing things as such and suches in general, but they have not *learned* to see the object in a relevant way, then we might legitimately say that they are *caused* to see the object as one thing rather than another, because of its pattern and the direction of its movement. That is not to say, of course, that they see it as a hawk or as a goose, but rather that they see it as whatever causes in them the respective reaction.

But the conditions which have to be satisfied if they are rightly to be said to see things as such and suches in general are, amongst other things, that they be concept possessors and users. This is not to say that they must have concepts *before* they see anything as a such and such. Seeing-as logically presupposes concept possession, but that fact has no implications about temporality. The only thing that cannot be the case is that the seeing-as precedes *any* kind of possession whatever of the relevant concepts. But concepts and seeing-as may certainly come together. With that arises the possibility of further learning, through interplay of concepts and experience. So, if the geese mentioned above are rightly to be said to see the pattern as one thing rather than another, they must either then or before that time have relevant concepts; and by 'relevant' here is meant 'relevant to their differential reaction or behaviour'. But because concepts are not atomic, and because of the 'network dependence' of which Woodfield speaks, seeing something as X in a way which implies that the concept of X comes with the perception is likely to involve the principle that the new experience and the new understanding must fit in with a pre-existing network. Are we any nearer to an understanding of how that network itself arises?[10]

Doubt about this may possibly seem to make the doctrine of innate concepts more attractive. There is, however, one consideration which should remove that attractiveness. Woodfield speaks of 'an inferentially integrated network *like our own*' (my italics). It is perfectly true that if there is to be mutual understanding and common knowledge there must be a common system of concepts, and, as Wittgenstein insisted, common ways of applying them (what he called 'agreement in judgments'). Hence if I were to say that the geese discussed above see the object as a hawk, and mean that seriously, I should have to presume in them a system of concepts which had some similarity to mine.

But we need not presume quite so much. If animals have concepts, we need not presume a great deal of similarity between their concepts and ours, although when we make their behaviour intelligible to ourselves it is natural for us to invoke concepts which we use in relation to ourselves. (We speak of dogs wanting a walk or trying to bury a bone – concepts which, taken at their face value, imply many other concepts which we may have no right to apply in their case.) The community of concepts is a condition of the possibility of communication, and of knowledge to the extent that the content of the imputed knowledge presupposes at least the possibility of its being communicated. Common knowledge – knowledge in Popper's 'third world' sense[11] – is something that cannot be entered into without shared concepts, but we can assume that animals have these, if only to the extent that they share with us common reactions to the world – in Wittgenstein's words, a common form of life.

As indicated in chapter 3, it has been argued by Tyler Burge, as an extension of Putnamian arguments, that social considerations may enter into questions about the meaning of terms. It is questionable, however, whether any arguments of that kind could sustain the thesis that the very fact of concept possession demands a social context in which the possessor must participate. There is, however, a further consideration which I have brought to bear on these matters elsewhere,[12] and which is no doubt derived ultimately from Wittgenstein. This is to the effect that someone cannot be a knower if he has no idea of what it is for things to be so or not so, or if he has no idea of what it is to be right or wrong. But it is difficult, indeed impossible, to see how someone could acquire the understanding of what it is to be right or wrong except in a social context, where he is subject to correction by others. But to see the force of such correction by others it is necessary to stand to them in certain sorts of relations, not all of which are purely cognitive. For what must be conveyed is a sense of why such things matter, and that presupposes feelings on our part as well as on theirs.

One way of putting this is to say that the concept of truth or its analogue, the possession of which to some degree or other is a condition of being a knower, brings with it the concept of conformity to a norm. Some might reject this, insisting that truth means only something like correspondence to the facts, and that it is a straightforward matter of fact whether that holds good.[13] Yet someone who knew that, but had no conception of whether or why that mattered, would surely have a very deficient grasp of the concept of truth. This is because into the idea of the attainment of truth there enters that of being right, and into its opposite there enters the idea of being wrong or of being in error. All these ideas presuppose for their attainment and acquisition a social context.

It is tempting to express the consequences of this by saying that, as a result, we should not consider as the system which is the subject-matter of cognitive psychology that which is comprised by the human individual, but rather that comprised by the society or at least the group of which he is a member. This might suggest in turn that individual psychology is to be reduced to social psychology. But that would clearly be a mistake. No story about social interactions alone can be adequate for an understanding of an individual's various capacities and of his behaviour in relation to the non-social environment. It is a fact, I suggest, that a new-born child abandoned on a desert island could never become a knower (it is most unlikely that it would even survive, for various reasons some of them connected with the fact that it could never be a knower[14]). But that does not mean that those who do become knowers are not individuals; they should be considered accordingly, whatever the context to which, as knowers or at least sometime knowers, they necessarily belong. They have individual capacities, nervous systems, and minds. Yet, if we thought it necessary to isolate the system to which reference has to be made in explaining human knowledge, we should have to specify, not just the organism in its relation to its physical environment, but that together with the social structure of which the individual is a part.

It is important in this to be clear that I am not just saying that it is important to recognize that human beings are social creatures. Piaget, who has tended to think of psychological development in terms of relations between the human organism and its environment (for example, in terms of such notions as assimilation and accommodation, as previously noted), has sometimes been criticized for insufficient emphasis upon social considerations. He has equally been defended against this accusation by followers, who have pointed out that he has had in fact much concern with social psychology, although this is not commonly known because the works in which he has discussed such matters have not been translated into English. But this is not in fact to the point. It is rather that the interrelations between the individual and the environment which are involved in knowledge of that environment *presuppose* a social existence; it is not that such interrelations are themselves essentially social. Hence the reference to the social in an account of the individual's acquisition of knowledge of the world, and in an explanation of the very possibility of that (which is, I believe, what Piaget ought to mean by what he calls 'genetic epistemology'), must come in at the beginning and not after the time at which knowledge already exists.

All this should serve to indicate why an appeal to innate concepts will not do in an explanation of concept acquisition or of the possibility of human learning. For, given what I have said, the idea of innate concepts, presupposing as it does that of innate knowledge, is incoherent. The only way out of that incoherence is to suppose, with Plato, in the *Meno* at least, that the innate knowledge is the product of experience in another life. For that experience could then have a social context (although that is not a point with which Plato himself has anything to do). Such a view would, however, generate its own incoherence, because it would lead to an infinite regress of innate knowledges depending on previous social existences. There is no recourse but to abandon the idea of innate knowledge altogether, and to explain the possibility of the acquisition of concepts and of new knowledge without it.

This equally entails an account of what concept acquisition involves which is different from that offered by, for example, Fodor. We must get away from the idea of the child using just the same procedures as the adult who seeks confirmation of his theories. Concept acquisition is not the use of abduction or anything like that. What it does involve is a fairly complex matter – both the interaction between concepts and experience which is involved in learning and also causal processes which, given the requisite background, bring it about that the individual sees things as such and such. (I have said nothing in this about what language makes possible. Although children learn much and, I believe, against many other philosophers, acquire concepts before they can talk, the actual acquisition of language has an effect which may be dramatic, to put it at its lowest. Moreover, the accounts of the acquisition of language which are currently on offer from psychologists and linguists seem in general simplistic and relatively simple-minded.)

What I have said about the necessity for a social existence at the beginning of the individual's cognitive life, when understanding begins, adds an additional complication to 'the effect of the past' on the individual's present cognitive state and its relation to the world in which he or she lives. An appeal to the idea of the storage of information is far from adequate for these purposes. If there is no way of avoiding appeal to the idea of knowledge in these matters – and I think that there is not (certainly not by appeal to the idea of tacit knowledge, which either retains the reference to knowledge proper or seeks rescue in as-if-ness) – the complexity of the system of concepts required to do justice to the cognitive states of human beings is way beyond anything that can be provided by an information-processing story alone. I shall in the next chapter turn to a brief consideration of what is in those terms the output side of the system, and we shall see that some of the same issues arise again.

7

Output

WHAT IS BEHAVIOUR?

Since a main concern of my study of cognition so far has been the extent to which cognition can plausibly be understood in information-processing terms, it may be wondered at this stage why it is necessary to consider output as well. It might be said that the output will be whatever results from the central processes, and from the point of view of cognition its nature does not matter very much. The output which results from such processes as are necessary to set up the central states corresponding to belief and so on is not a matter of great interest for one concerned primarily with those central states. All that we need to assume is that those central states cause some form of output, which in most cases will consist of some form of bodily movement. Such a view would be a mistake, however, although I believe it is commonly held among those concerned to explain in information-processing terms the way in which human beings come to have beliefs about the world. Apart from anything else, there is the fact, on which I have laid emphasis, that a full understanding of perception is impossible without the recognition of the part played in it by agency.

It will be remembered that this book began with a discussion of behaviourism, because, it was claimed, the theoretical point of view of cognitive psychology emerged from and was in a sense parasitical on that of behaviourism. According to behaviourism in its most basic form, all behaviour is ultimately analysable into stimulus–response connections. I pointed out the ambiguity that underlies both the terms involved – stimulus and response. If I am right in suggesting that the theoretical basis of cognitive psychology derived from the attempt to fill in the gap between stimulus and response and then to put certain refinements upon how the stimulus side was to be construed (that is, the information-processing story), one cannot, if one is to arrive at an adequate appraisal of that, simply ignore the response side. The information-processing story, for example, would have no plausibility if it did not make possible an account of how there can take place forms of output which are relevant to the input and can be seen as possible in its terms. Simply to brandish the notion of causality, and say that, just as central states are caused to exist by the input processes, whatever their nature, so they in turn cause output is not good enough.

Suppose, for example, that it was thought sufficient to construe the output of that system which makes up the human organism in terms of a multiplicity of muscle-movements. The question would then arise about the relevance of any information processing that takes place to those muscle-movements; indeed, given that kind of output, questions of relevance would arise with respect to central processes construed in any terms other than purely physiological ones. The same thing would hold good the other way round. Given a certain construal of the central processes, what construal of the output itself could then be considered relevant? What kind of output would one expect to be relevant to, say, central processes which are of a computational kind? It is difficult to know what sort of answer one could give to that question. If, then, it *were* possible to explain all central processes in computational terms, one would not by any means have won the whole battle. It would still be necessary to provide an understanding of how they are related to an output construed in a way which makes psychological sense. In the end that means showing how it relates to behaviour. It would have to explain why, given forms of perception and a variety of central processes, human beings do what they do in various circumstances. What is the relevance of computational processes to that?

One putative, though only partial, answer to that question might be that some of the processes in question have to do with representations; when behaviour occurs, it does so in the light of such representations. Apart from the doubts which I have already expressed about the whole notion of representations in general and that of the representational theory of the mind in particular, it could be said that an appeal to representations at this point is something of a fraud; the appeal is made simply to provide an otherwise missing connection between the central processes and behaviour. This might be thought too severe a judgement. But those who preach an eliminative approach to the psychology of cognition, suggesting that a folk-psychological reference to such things as beliefs should be eliminated by any self-respecting scientific psychology, ought also to maintain that psychology should have nothing to do with behaviour either. On the other hand, those who, like Fodor, see themselves as defenders of folk psychology, but nevertheless favour an appeal to computational processes, even if combined with an appeal to representations, should also make clear exactly what they see folk psychology as explaining on the output side.

What, then, is behaviour? Some years ago it was received doctrine that 'behaviour' is synonymous with 'action', and that action, even bodily action, is not to be analysed in terms of bodily movements. It was taken to be a corollary of this that action could not be explained in the terms appropriate to the occurrence of bodily movements. In particular it was not to be explained in terms of causes, as seems possible with the occurrence of bodily movements. The climate of philosophical opinion changed in this respect with the publication of Donald Davidson's 'Actions, reasons and causes'.[1] Davidson was taken to have shown that, so far from it being the case that the explanation of an action in terms of the reasons for it excludes there being causes of such action, reasons are themselves causes of action. It was claimed that an action was standardly to be explained in terms of a pro-attitude or want in respect of some object, combined with a belief that the action in question was necessary for the attainment of the object and for the satisfaction of the want. Davidson argued, in a way that it is unnecessary to go into here, that an appeal to such things, although not under those descriptions, was to give the causes of the action. (Strictly speaking, this did not show that reasons were causes; rather it showed at best that the *having of a reason* could be construed as the cause of the relevant action, but for present purposes this point can be ignored.)

It does not directly follow from the fact, if it is one, that actions can be explained in terms of causes, that action can be analysed in terms of bodily movements. For one thing, as has been made clear by Jennifer Hornsby,[2] there is a distinction to be made

between a transitive and an intransitive sense of 'bodily movement'. In the former sense a bodily movement is *made* by someone, and is for that reason tantamount to a particular kind of
action; it can, for example, be intentional. In the sense in which
Davidson suggested that a complex of beliefs and wants explain
an action by giving its cause it constitutes the cause of bodily
movements only in the transitive sense of that term. Or rather,
the beliefs and wants constitute an intelligible cause and provide
an intelligible explanation only in that case. For it is undeniable
that, when we *make* a bodily movement, a bodily movement in
the intransitive sense occurs; when we move an arm certain arm
movements take place. But we should expect an explanation of
the latter to be provided by reference to other physiological
occurrences, not, or not directly, by reference to beliefs and
wants.

The term 'behaviour' involves a similar ambiguity to the one
which applies to 'bodily movement'. We speak of the behaviour
of inanimate objects, from physical particles to machines, via,
say, the weather. Some philosophers have supposed that it is in
the same sense of 'behaviour' that we speak of human behaviour,
and I indicated in discussing behaviourism that the proponents of
that theory make more or less the same presumption. But the
output which is to be explained by reference to central cognitive
processes or the perceptual processes which, as input, lead to
these is not behaviour in that sense. The behaviour which is
explained by reference to how we see things, what we conse-
quently believe, and so on, is a form of action, whether or not
that kind of explanation is one which is causal. There is indeed an
important but often overlooked note (note 2) to the article by
Davidson mentioned earlier which makes clear, not only that he
sees his concern as being with actions, but also that the notion of
an action is related to what can be considered intentional.

ACTION AND INTENTION

The view that actions are to be explained by reference to beliefs
and wants or desires has become almost *de rigueur* among those
concerned with the philosophy of action. It is quite often
suggested, to be more explicit, that we always explain actions by

saying that the actor wants some end and believes that performing this action, doing this thing, will bring about that end. It
would in fact be at least an exaggeration to say that all actions are
to be explained in this way. Such a view presupposes that all
actions are done as means to some end, and that none are done
for their own sake or for no particular reason. In any case, the
view in question presumes that the actions in question are intentional, since unintentional actions, which are surely still actions
even if not intentional ones, are clearly not done because the
actor wants something and believes that this action will bring
about what he wants. The question then arises what makes the
actions intentional when they are; it can scarcely be that the agent
wants something and believes that doing this will bring about
what he wants. In any case, Davidson himself has pointed out, as
indeed have some others, that there may be occasions on which
someone does something because he wants something and believes that doing this will bring about that thing, but the action is
unintentional. In that case the action is caused by a conjunction
of beliefs and desires but not in the way in which a corresponding
intentional action is caused.

This has generated a plethora of inquiries into what have
become known as 'deviant causal chains' (ways in which beliefs
and desires cause actions, but not in the way in which they are
supposed to do when the actions are intentional), in spite of the
fact that Davidson himself expressed pessimism about solving the
problem. Let us try to see in a little more detail what the problem
is. Davidson presented it in a paper entitled 'Freedom to act'.[3]
The example on which it all turns is that of a climber who
supports another man on a rope; he wants to get rid of the other
man, and the thought occurs to him that if he lets go the rope that
result will be achieved. That thought so unnerves him that he
loosens his hold and the man does fall. In that case, it is said, the
combination of desire and belief does cause the result, in spite of
the fact that the action of loosening hold on the rope is unintentional. It seems to follow from this that it cannot be that an
action's being brought about by certain causes is what makes it an
intentional action.

It might of course be said that in this sort of case the action is
brought about causally by the belief and desire in a different way
from the norm, and subsequent work on 'deviant causal chains'[4]

includes attempts to spell out what is involved in this idea of a 'different way'. Whether this can be done successfully is not my present concern. What is more important for present purposes is that it appears from all this that it is more plausible to maintain that the intentional character of an action is in fact *presupposed* in the attempt to explain that action by reference to beliefs and desires; its being intentional is not determined by that causal background.[5]

Davidson makes some relevant remarks on the issue in the Introduction to his *Essays on Actions and Events*, p. xiii, but I believe that he goes in the wrong direction. He says that when he wrote 'Actions, reasons and causes' he thought that 'of the three main uses of the concept of intention distinguished by Elizabeth Anscombe (acting with an intention, acting intentionally and intending to act) the first was the most basic'. He suggests that when he wrote the original paper he thought that acting intentionally was just acting with some intention. He now thinks that intending is the basic notion in terms of which the others are to be explained.[6] Whether this is a correct assessment of his position in the earlier paper is arguable, but it seems quite wrong to say that an action is intentional if and only if it is preceded or accompanied by an act of intending, whatever is involved in that. As I shall indicate later, there are many things done intentionally which do not presuppose a prior act of intending. What in any case would such an act be?

Davidson's answer to that question has a connection with the idea of a practical syllogism, as originally put forward by Aristotle. The theory of the practical syllogism is supposed to be one about the kinds of deliberative processes which underlie decisions about conduct. The deliberative processes are practical not only because they are concerned with what we should do, but also because they reflect the kinds of beliefs and wants which we have in the situation in question. Hence there is a connection between the practical syllogism and the idea that actions are to be explained in terms of complexes of beliefs and wants or desires.

The considerations which led to theses about 'deviant causal chains' have led Davidson, first and rightly, to the belief that an intention is not to be analysed simply in terms of such complexes of wants and desires, and, secondly and more controversially, to the belief that the idea of pure intending is paramount in this context. I am not concerned to dispute the claim that there are such things as pure intendings, although Schopenhauer, for one, thought that intentions for the future have by no means the same status as the intentions with which one performs one's current action. Apart from the considerations which have been taken to lead to the invocation of 'deviant causal chains', it is possible to argue that in certain circumstances one can form an intention to act in a way which transcends any wants or beliefs that one may have. It is possible to be asked to form such an intention and to act in accordance with it in a way which sets aside and disregards any wants or beliefs that one may have about one's action and its consequences.[7]

It is not normally like that, however, and actions which result from practical deliberation may normally result from the formation of an intention on the basis of considerations about one's wants and beliefs. That is where the idea of the practical syllogism comes in. Aristotle said, in a way that has puzzled commentators, that the conclusion of such a syllogism is an action, not merely the expression of an intention to act, or a judgement about what one should do. Whether or not one *should* be puzzled about the idea that a process of deliberation, involving premises about what is desirable and about the circumstances, may lead to an action rather than a conclusion about the appropriate action, practical deliberation does often lead to action.

Davidson's thought is that the last stage of the deliberation is an all-out judgement, as opposed to the conditional judgements which go into the considerations that are involved in the premises of the deliberative argument. He says at the end of his paper 'Intending', 'Pure intendings constitute a subclass of the all-out judgements, those directed to future actions of the agent, and made in the light of his beliefs' (*Essays*, p. 102). Intending and wanting 'belong to the same genus of pro-attitudes expressed by value judgements', but the value judgement involved in intending, which is a value judgement about the desirability of an action, is all-out or non-conditional, whereas that involved in wanting is conditional. When we act as the result of practical deliberation, the action follows directly because the judgement is all-out, and not merely conditional.

It is clear that some distinction such as that made between all-out and conditional judgements is required to put an end to considerations such as 'I want X, and believe that doing A will, in the circumstances which I believe to obtain, produce X; so, if I want X and believe these things, I must do A . . .' The conclusion of the deliberative process must, if it is to be effective, terminate in something which is not hedged around by 'ifs'. It is not clear, however, that that is what intending is. Just as the motivation of 'Actions, reasons and causes' was to reduce what is involved in acting from an intention to the causal role performed by complexes of beliefs and desires (something that emerged as implausible because of the considerations adduced in 'Freedom to act'), so in 'Intending' the motivation is to reduce pure intending, now claimed as basic because of the failure of the previous account, to something else, namely a class of value judgements. It might justly be said that this involves a failure to take the will seriously.

I said that I believed that in all this Davidson has gone in the wrong direction. Apart from doubts about the reductive strategy followed in general by Davidson, there should be scepticism about the claim that we should seek an understanding of all intentional action by reference to the role played by pure intendings, however construed. It may be more profitable, and I believe that it is in fact so, to go back to the idea of intentional action or of acting intentionally, which has been neglected so far. Not all actions which are done intentionally are done with an intention or for a further intention, let alone as the result of a pure intending. There are many things which we do with nothing further in mind with regard to them; yet we may well do them intentionally. We may do them for no particular reason, but they are done, and they are not done unintentionally. What is crucial to their intentional status is that they are done knowingly.

To say that is not to provide an analysis of intentional action, or to spell out one of the components into which that is to be reduced. For one thing, the knowledge in question is a knowledge of what is done *in acting*. Various philosophers have tried to specify what that kind of knowledge amounts to, saying that it is, for example, practical knowledge or knowledge without observation; but such specifications tend to be insufficient, either because the specification itself cannot be explained without reference to what it specifies (as with the idea of practical knowledge) or because the specification is too wide to delimit the class it purports to specify (as with the idea of knowledge without observation).[8] It nevertheless remains true that an action which is performed intentionally is done knowingly in some sense.

SUB-INTENTIONAL ACTION

It ought to follow from what I have just said that if an action was done but not done knowingly it cannot have been done intentionally. It does not follow immediately from that that it was done unintentionally, unless there is no such thing as an action performed non-intentionally, so that the class of actions is exhaustively divided between those that are intentional and those that are unintentional. There are two points which are perhaps worthy of mention in this connection. First, Aristotle, in *Nicomachean Ethics*, III. 1, discusses the distinction between voluntary and involuntary actions (if these terms represent adequate translations of the Greek *hekōn* and *akōn*), in connection with the questions when people are responsible for their actions and when they should be praised or blamed for them. He discusses, among other things, the question when ignorance makes the action involuntary (and we might ask whether that means the same as 'unintentional'), and he says that ignorance of the particular circumstances of the action makes that action involuntary only when there is subsequent regret or remorse.

Aristotle has come under criticism for this claim on the grounds that something that occurs after the event cannot surely affect its status as intentional or unintentional. But is that right? After all a person might well in these circumstances say 'I did not mean (intend) to do *that*', and others might agree on that verdict. On the other hand, if he did not repent of the action, it could be said of him that he wanted what he brought about all the time. But did he *intend* it, did he do whatever he did *intentionally*? Perhaps he would have intended the result, had he known he would be producing it, but did he actually intend it, as things were? He did not, after all, do what he did knowingly. It *does* seem to be the case that in that event he didn't actually do what he did intentionally, although because it appears from the non-repentance that he wanted the result we might perhaps say that he did what he did willingly or voluntarily. If that is so, the connection between intentional action and knowledge must be retained. Moreover, in doing what he did in ignorance, he did that thing in particular unintentionally, however welcome the result was. There is no need here to posit a class of non-intentional action; rather, we need additional categories of unintentional action.

The other point is that in the process of complex activities like driving a car we perform many actions by, as it were, rote, without thinking what we are doing. Are such actions intentional or not? The same considerations apply to things done out of habit. They are scarcely done knowingly – or are they? Brian O'Shaughnessy refers to such actions as sub-intentional actions.[9] If such a categorization is acceptable, it might be suggested that we have at least one kind of non-intentional action which is not thereby unintentional. For it seems evident that the complex actions performed in the course of driving a car successfully cannot be said to be unintentional – not all of them at any rate. However, I do not think that it follows from the fact that such acts were performed without the person concerned thinking of them that they were not performed knowingly. The person may not have been conscious of doing them, although he was no doubt conscious of performing some broader category of action, such as driving the car. That is to say that he was conscious of what he was doing under that broader description, but not perhaps under the description 'turning the wheel slightly to the left, then to the right'.

Did he *know* what he was doing under that latter description? Perhaps not, but that is because to know something under a certain description is to be aware of it under that description, and the question at issue is whether it is possible to know what one is doing in general without being aware of that. What seems clear is that the person whom we are considering knew what he was doing in general, and that the possession of a skill requires both that and the ability to do what is necessary for the performance of the skill. So there is a sense in which he turned the wheel knowingly without thinking explicitly of what he was doing. If that is so he turned the wheel intentionally and there is no need *on these grounds* to posit a category of sub-intentional action. *A fortiori*, there is no need on these grounds for a category of non-intentional action.

It is important to note in this connection that doing something knowingly does not entail doing it consciously. That it does not entail that is indeed implicit in what I have said about there being no need for a category of sub-intentional action; for the argument for such a category of actions depends upon the point that one may do certain things without being explicitly conscious of doing so. Some philosophers in the phenomenological tradition have argued that knowledge in general entails knowing that one knows; and Sartre has insisted, in conformity with his general conception of a *pour soi*, as opposed to the *en soi*, on an even stronger thesis – that knowing entails being conscious that one knows. There is little to be said for either thesis.

There are many cases in which it would be right to say that someone knows something but in which for some reason (it might be inadvertence or a failure to put two and two together, for example) he clearly does not know that he does. The stock example in the philosophical literature is that of the reluctant schoolboy, of whom a teacher may be quite certain that he knows the answer to some question, but the boy does not acknowledge the fact and may be, for some reason, reluctant to do so. Again, we ourselves may discover that we know some fact and have known it for some time, without knowing that we do. If it is thus possible for us to know something without knowing that we do, it is *a fortiori* possible, to an even greater extent, for us to know something without being conscious of doing so. We can equally do things knowingly without being conscious of the fact that we are doing so.[10]

Does what has been said about sub-intentional action apply also to habits in general? Not necessarily, but that does not affect the question of the existence of non-intentional action. The reason for concluding that a component of a skill could be considered to be an intentional action was just that it *was* a component of a skill; it was part of something that was in general done knowingly. Not all habits are like that. We sometimes perform some isolated act out of habit, because something in the circumstances sparks it off and we act without thinking. Suppose that the question then arose whether we intended to do what was done. There was no forethought nor thought at the time; there was nothing in the context of the action which suggests that in general we knew what we were up to, indeed the description of what happened precludes that. So, if the question of whether the action was intentional arose the answer would be likely to be

'No'. Once again there is no case for speaking of sub-intentional action, and there is no case for speaking of non-intentional action either. Circumstances will determine whether it is right to say that the action was intentional or unintentional, and it will be one or the other.

AGENCY AND KNOWLEDGE

It has been argued by, for example, Davidson that if an action is unintentional under one description it will be intentional under some other description. This thesis is at first sight extremely plausible. If one does something in ignorance of what one is doing, one is nevertheless performing an action. One did not mean to do *that*, but is there not something which one meant to do? Yet if we do something out of habit, and thereby do something which we did not mean to do, so that the action is by my reckoning unintentional, it does not seem to be the case that there was anything which was done intentionally, even if under another description. The only thing that was done was done unintentionally. If that is right, it cannot be true that everything that is done is done knowingly under some description. Knowledge does not enter directly into everything that we do. On the other hand, and in a more general sense, it is very unclear how someone could act unintentionally out of habit unless he was in general capable of doing things intentionally, indeed unless he actually did some things intentionally. If that is so, an actor must be a knower (and, given what I said in an earlier chapter about perception and agency, vice versa). But that is not to say that every action involves knowledge, although many, perhaps most, will.

What I have just said provides a general reflection upon the notion of agency. It is one of the great merits of Schopenhauer that he had a profound insight into the importance of that notion. In the general context of his philosophy what he called 'will' had a meaning and scope which is far wider than anything that can justifiably be brought under the heading of agency, but his argument for all that starts from the fact of agency, and in particular from the fact that in action we, as human beings, can know in a direct and unconditioned way that we are acting. We cannot have such knowledge of anything else, nor indeed of the motives for our actions which give those actions their identity. We can thus know in a direct and unconditioned way that we are doing something, but *what* we do cannot be so known.[11] Nevertheless, something is an action only if it can be known as such, and thereby the general and essential connection, in the context of agency, between knowledge and action becomes apparent. Agents must be knowers.

Given what I said in the last chapter about the conditions of knowledge, this has very considerable implications both for an understanding of what is involved in action and how we are to construe the system that makes up a human being capable of action. For one thing, if it is the case that only a social being can have knowledge it follows that only a social being can act. If that is right, it underlines even more the fact that the nature of the output of any cognitive system which has any similarity to a human being is not an obvious and simple matter. Nor can it simply be taken as read. A full account of a cognitive being must take into account not only how what is derived from the use of the sense-organs is processed and related to central processes; it must also consider how that cognitive being relates to other such beings in such a way as to enable it to acquire the idea of what it is to be right and wrong, and only in the light of that can we understand what it is for it to be capable of doing anything.

It might be thought that the claim that only a social being can act raises even greater problems for understanding the development of a human being from birth than do the more straightforward epistemological issues discussed in the previous chapter. How are we to understand what the new-born baby 'does' if that is not to be taken as action in the full sense – as must be the case given that such a baby is not as yet a social being? The answer must be along the lines of the previous discussion of the development of concept possession and use. The knowledge that is presupposed by the possibility of agency is still a matter of degree. There will be no first moment at which it will be clear that the child is an agent; indeed there will be no first moment at which it will be right to say that now he or she is an agent. The system will initially react to the environment according to its principles of organization. But a human child is not just a biological system, nor just an information-processing system. It is capable of responding with feeling to similar behaviour on the part of others, and from this emerges what is necessary for the possibility of knowledge, and in that context reactions become actions.

I do not claim in that to have given any adequate account of what happens. All that I do claim is that a child is not in any proper sense an agent unless and until it is a knower; it is not *that* unless and until it has some sense of what it is to be right and wrong, correct and incorrect; it cannot acquire that except via a context of relations with others which presuppose feeling, not just states of mind which are purely cognitive (if there is any such thing, which I think, for reasons spelled out earlier, there cannot be). But it must be born with the capacity to develop feelings, to respond to input processes which, while causal, may also come to be taken as information-bearing, and to react to the environment so perceived in ways which, given the satisfaction of the other conditions mentioned, may make those reactions actions.

We are far from understanding all that, or indeed its possibility, even when that is taken at the level at which I have so far described it. We are even further from having any appreciation in any kind of detail of the kinds of mechanism which make it possible. But it is no good speculating about the kinds of processes underlying the receipt of information about the world in perception, or the central processes which both result from them and make them possible, if the resulting story does not make intelligible the possibility of action, or explain output in terms which are psychologically relevant and well-founded. Agency is a puzzling phenomenon, to put the matter in the most basic and least tendentious terms; but it cannot be ignored or explained away.

In the light of all this let us go back to the question how, if a human being is to be treated as a cognitive system, the output is to be categorized. To repeat – it is no good simply saying that the output is whatever is caused by the central states, not even if it is added that it consists of bodily movements. For we do not, and could not, understand the kind of connection which might hold between, for example, a belief and a set of bodily movements which happen to take place when it ensues. And the same applies to any information-bearing state. That is not to say that there is no connection, but it is an extremely indirect one.

It is no doubt the case that such bodily movements are in a

particular case the effect of complex physiological processes that are taking place in the human being construed as an organism (unless, of course, there are instances where physiological causes are insufficient, and appeal to some mental cause is required – but I lay no weight on that, apparently empirical, possibility). If token cognitive states are realized in such physiological states and processes, then they are on this occasion the cause of the bodily movements that occur. But this affords us no understanding of the connection, if any, between types of cognitive states and types of bodily movement, as is necessary if they are to explain them. But we do think that there is a connection between, on the one hand, wanting something and believing that doing such and such will bring it about, and, on the other, a certain kind of action. That is one way, but, as I have been anxious to point out, not the only way, in which we think an action is to be explained.[12]

Only if output is construed as action can we make psychological sense of it. But in that case the person in question must be capable of, at the least, doing things intentionally. This in turn implies that he must be a knower, and that implies all the things that I have set out as conditions of knowledge. He must be a social being, who is capable thereby of appreciating the force of a norm (as is implicit in seeing things as so or not so). Finally, for this to be so he cannot be a purely cognitive being. Things must matter for him, and this depends upon what can be described only as feeling.

8

Conclusion

Those who are opposed to physicalist approaches to the mind (and most contemporary cognitive scientists provide examples of such approaches) often claim that the primary objections to such approaches derive from the general nature of intentionality.[1] This point is put in different ways by different critics, but it is the 'of-ness' or 'about-ness' of certain mental states, the fact that they are concerned with objects, whether real or not, or, as it is sometimes put, the fact that they mean things and thereby have a semantics, that is held to constitute the crucial problem. There is much in what I have said in this book which echoes that point. It should also be clear, however, that there are certain other points which arise in this connection, and it is arguable that they are more fundamental. I have mentioned these points in the foregoing, but it would be useful to underline them again here in this final chapter.

There is, first, the point that in connection with what has come to be called cognition, despite certain philosophers' objections to the term on the grounds of its woolliness, it is knowledge, rather than belief, which is the fundamental notion. In our dealings with the world it would be of little point to have beliefs unless such beliefs were often true. Provided that such beliefs were true our dealings with the world would be successful, whatever it is that success consists in. But, as Plato insisted in his *Meno*, while true beliefs get you to the right results just because they are true, there is a sense in which they are not by themselves reliable. Plato seems to suggest that this is because they are not likely to be firmly implanted, but this is not really the main point.

The important thing is that there is nothing in the nature of belief by itself which ensures that a belief will be true; truth depends on things outside the belief, in particular on whether it corresponds to the facts. If a belief is well-founded it has a good chance, though not an absolute certainty, of being true to the facts. Whether or not the traditional account of knowledge as justified true belief is satisfactory (and there has been a whole industry of attempts in recent times to show that it is not and to decide in consequence what should be done about it), it is certainly the case that, if it is a mere accident that we attain the truth, this will make any beliefs we have to that effect far from well-founded. Indeed, it has sometimes been suggested with at least considerable plausibility that for a belief to constitute knowledge it must be no accident that it is the truth that is believed.

I am not concerned here to argue whether a 'no accident' view of knowledge is adequate to explain what knowledge is. What is important for present purposes is that our dealings with the world must, for success, depend on more than mere accident. That is in effect Plato's point. But one way of taking what he then says is simply that we have to ensure that our true beliefs are stable. We have to ensure that such beliefs of ours as are true do not slip from our mind, to be replaced perhaps by beliefs which are false. It is far from clear that that idea, by itself, will do. Would it be adequate, for example, if there were some arrangement, the guidance of a God perhaps, which ensured that we usually acquired and retained true beliefs, without our having to do anything to work out what was true and why? (Indeed, on the orthodox interpretation of Plato's text, he makes Socrates go on to insist that true beliefs are to be turned into knowledge by working out the reasons for them; but the connection between that suggestion and the point about the instability of true beliefs is not altogether clear.)

It might be argued that in the case which I have contemplated, involving the guidance of a God, it would in fact be no accident that it is the truth that we believe; whatever it is that ensures that we believe the truth brings it about by that very means that it is no accident that it is the truth that we believe. In that respect the agency of a God would be in the same position as a totally reliable causal mechanism. Indeed, some philosophers have suggested that an appeal to such a reliable causal mechanism is what is wanted, rather than an appeal to justifying reasons, in an account of what turns belief into knowledge. In fact, the probability is that whether we should appeal to reliable causal mechanisms or justifying reasons, or indeed anything else, depends on the case under consideration. Certainly there are cases of knowledge, for example the knowledge of where a limb of ours currently is, where an appeal to justifying reasons does not seem to the point; there are equally cases, for example the knowledge of mathematical truths, where there do not seem to be causal connections between the fact and the belief. What matters is that *something* should rule out the belief being true by luck or accident. It remains a question whether, for knowledge, that is all that matters.[2]

It remains far from clear whether a creature which had reliable and stable beliefs, however these were produced, but had no ability to assess those and any other beliefs could properly be said to be a knower. Another way of putting that point is to ask what, in that case, the beliefs themselves would amount to. To have a belief is to hold something as true, and with that appeal to truth a normative idea is introduced, which rules out the purely naturalistic account which seems to be presupposed by the idea that it is sufficient to appeal to a reliable causal origin for the beliefs. A God could cause us to have true beliefs via the fact that he himself knows the truth; a reliable causal mechanism could cause us to have true beliefs only if we were capable of true belief anyway, and being capable of that surely presupposes being able to *assess* questions about truth. That in turn involves being able to judge what sort of thing counts in favour of truth and what sort of thing does not. A plausible way of putting that is to say that belief presupposes knowledge. It is not of course that the belief that p presupposes knowledge that p, but that belief that p presupposes knowledge of *some* kind, and indeed knowledge that is in some way relevant to p (though relevance may be totally a matter of degree).

I suggest, then, that we cannot have stable true beliefs unless we are in some sense knowers. When we say that someone or something is a knower, we are not simply passing a normative judgement, saying that he, she or it has reached a certain standard which justifies the ascription of knowledge, although we are doing that among other things. We imply also that the creature in question is capable of assessing such things itself, whether or not it does so on a specific occasion. To that extent being a knower and being rational go hand in hand (something that does not of course rule out the possibility of irrational behaviour on the part of a knower, at any rate on occasion). There are indeed a cluster of concepts which go together in their applicability to creatures – those of knowledge, rationality, the capacity for learning, for example. That one of these is applied on a particular occasion does not entail that the others have to be applied on the same occasion. Apart from the points which I have already mentioned, it may be pointed out, as I did in an earlier chapter, that someone can come to know certain things without this being by learning; but he could not do so if he were incapable of learning altogether.

All this puts a very high premium on the notion of knowledge and these related concepts. It also casts doubt on the idea of an intentional state taken by itself, despite the number of occasions on which I have referred to such an idea in the foregoing. I do not by that mean that the notion of intentionality is itself wrong; nor do I mean that there are no such things as beliefs and desires, which can plausibly be said to be intentional and, with qualifications as regards their identity as states, to constitute intentional states. Beliefs, however identified, are about things; they are to the effect that such and such is the case. Similarly, desires are for things and may be desires that such and such be the case. Moreover, as Brentano insisted, we may have beliefs and desires whether or not their objects exist, and whether or not what we believe or desire holds good objectively or as a fact of nature. So there are certainly intentional states by such criteria. The point is rather that such intentional states presuppose that those who have them are knowers also. So it is wrong to see the main objections to cognitive science or an information-processing model of cognitive psychology as stemming from intentionality alone. They stem from what lies at the back of that – the fact that human beings and some animals are knowers too.

But the conditions which have to be satisfied if something is to be a knower, that is to say the conditions for the possibility of that, need emphasis also. I have mentioned them all earlier, but they require emphasis yet again. First, to be a knower something must appreciate the force of what it is for things to be so and not so; it must appreciate the force of what it is to be right and wrong. To the extent that this involves an appreciation of the idea of truth, it means that truth and parallel notions are normative notions. Hence, anything that is an actual or potential knower must appreciate in some way and to some extent (once again this can be totally a matter of degree) the force of a norm. This does not entail appreciating, let alone accepting, any particular norm; it involves simply an understanding of what a norm is.

It might fairly be objected that this involves knowledge too; so am I not saying that knowledge presupposes knowledge? In a sense I *am*, but, as I have insisted elsewhere,[3] this does not mean that the one item of knowledge has to come before the other. It means only that if something is to have knowledge at all a number of different items must be in the package. There is no way, however, in which something could come to appreciate the force of a norm by itself, without the idea of a norm being in some way imposed upon it. This implies that a knower must have a social context of some kind. It follows that it is wrong to think of the system which is under consideration, when we are concerned with the receipt of information, its processing, and action in accordance with that, as one that is confined to the individual, however much one can restrict one's attention to the individual for certain specific purposes.[4]

These points also bring in the second condition which anything that is an actual or possible knower must satisfy. This too has already been mentioned. It is that the appreciation of the force of a norm and the appreciation of its imposition by others cannot be a purely cognitive matter. That this is so is implicit in the ideas of a 'force' and of 'imposition'. These entail attitudes on our part when we so appreciate them. To have an attitude towards something implies in turn our having certain feelings towards it as an object. It is no doubt true that the majority of attitudes and of the corresponding feelings or emotions have a cognitive element. This has been emphasized by numerous philosophers writing on the emotions in recent years, but the idea goes back at least as far as the Stoics. Indeed, some philosophers have suggested that emotions can be analysed entirely into cognitive elements. That seems exceedingly implausible, and would indeed entirely empty the idea of the emotions of anything that was distinctive of them. That, however, does not preclude the idea that most emotions have a cognitive element.

Nor does it preclude the idea, not that all or most instances of cognition have an emotive element (for there is nothing wrong with the idea of purely dispassionate knowledge), but that cognition in general depends for its possibility in the individual on that individual having feelings. That in turn means that the application of the computational metaphor (which I assume has nothing to do with feelings) implies at best a restricted system of information receipt and use, and not by any means the whole of it. It cannot of itself provide a complete understanding of what such information receipt and use involves. The thought that a cognitive science, relying more or less exclusively on that computational metaphor and taking it seriously, can stand on its own feet is therefore a mistaken one. That is not to say that an appeal to computational processes has no utility at all in this area. It is merely to say that it should not be too imperialistic; it should not lay claim to the whole truth, and the question how much of the truth it can lay claim to is still very uncertain.

The third condition that should be mentioned in this context is implicit in what I said in an earlier chapter about perception and agency, but it has wider scope than was implied there. For the idea of a purely passive knower, who has to do nothing to get knowledge but to wait until the knowledge is produced in him, is a scarcely credible one, and is altogether incredible if a sufficiently wide conception of 'doing' is allowed. Part of the argument for the thesis that a perceiver must be an agent turned on the idea that a perceiver must have some form of commerce with the world, which presupposes his doing things in relation to it. To the extent that knowledge depends on perception in one way or another that argument carries over to knowledge.

In a more general sense of 'doing', however, the requirement that a knower be a doer or agent follows from what I said earlier about the connection between knowledge and rationality. For, to be rational someone must be capable of assessing positions, of following out reasons, and possibly of being critical. All these things presuppose our not being merely passive in relation to putative objects of knowledge. The agency in question may not be physical agency but it is agency all the same. Pure passivity is incompatible with knowledge acquisition and possession. The question how the purely causal processes involved in sense perception and other forms of knowledge acquisition fit together with the idea that we are in various ways active is still an unanswered one. But that both these kinds of thing hold good of human beings seems indisputable. Once again, this imposes limits on the applicability of the computational metaphor.

It might be objected to all this that I have paid insufficient attention to the sub-personal. I have said a little about that in earlier chapters, but it would be only reasonable to acknowledge that I have given the sub-personal comparatively little weight. How much weight one *should* give to that notion is an arguable matter. Some appeals to the sub-personal involve reference to processes which are just like the processes which we may be conscious of engaging in as full-blooded persons. This applies, for example, to the idea of sub-doxastic states; they are supposed to be just like belief states except that we are not conscious of having them, and there is a sense in which they are not proper states of the person. On the other hand, it is undeniable that all sorts of processes may be going on when we engage in cognitive activity.

One may be able to get some purchase on what is possible here if we consider certain phenomena, where it may seem fairly evident that something has gone on in us which we are not aware of, but which is somehow directed towards the same ends as conscious and personal activity. I have in mind, in particular, the sort of thing which is reported as going on in some cases of mathematical thinking and which may go on in us in a lesser way in certain more or less intellectual activities, such as crossword-solving. Some aspects of the issue in connection with the solution of mathematical problems were noted by Henri Poincaré, and have been more extensively discussed by Jacques Hadamard.[5]

The psychology of thinking is a difficult area on which to be dogmatic, but there do seem to be circumstances in which one may report having thought of such and such during a certain interval of time without being able to report anything as having passed through or taken place in one's mind during that interval.[6] It may be, however, that such cases will be taken simply to raise questions about the concept of thinking itself. More crucial cases are those noted by Hadamard, in which, say, someone goes to bed with a mathematical problem which he cannot solve and wakes up with it solved. Has he been unconsciously continuing with the solution while asleep, or what?

It might be said that, given what is often said about dreams, we may continue with all sorts of mental processes while we are asleep and then do so unconsciously. Why therefore cannot it be the case that in the problem-solution example the people concerned carry on thinking about it unconsciously but in an otherwise full, personal sense? Is there any reason to invoke the category of the sub-personal here? Perhaps, and perhaps not. It is not in fact entirely clear what we should say. In other instances, however, when the solution to a problem comes to us after an interval during which we were entirely conscious and during which all our attention was on other things, it is not very plausible to say that we were at the same time thinking out the solution unconsciously. Rather, we might say, during that time the mechanism has been ticking over unbeknown to us, and at the end the solution to the problem has emerged. If that is right, the processes occurring are in a relatively clear sense sub-personal. I put the matter in terms of 'processes occurring', because it would be a quite different matter to say that the *thinking* was sub-personal. For that would imply that *we* were thinking sub-personally, or, in other words, that *a person was thinking sub-personally*. That would appear to involve a contradiction.

It might be objected that this is too strong a claim. The fact remains that if we attribute to a person processes, activities or states, which are supposed to be just like those which persons engage in or have, whether consciously or unconsciously, except that in this case the person in question does not, properly speaking, engage in or have them, this requires considerable justification. The issues here are similar to those that I raised over the idea of tacit knowledge. There is involved an extension of a concept from the place where the normal conditions for its application are satisfied to a place where they cannot be. As with the concept of tacit knowledge, it might be claimed that this simply parallels the extension of an everyday concept, such as that of energy, in a technical and theoretical way in physics. The difference, however, is that a concept such as that of thinking (and the same applies, not only to the activities of persons, but their states, such as belief and indeed knowledge) is essentially tied to that of a self or something akin to that.[7] For that reason, some, such as Dennett, who have wanted to posit sub-personal states or activities, have also had recourse to the idea of homunculi to be the owners of these states or the originators of these sub-personal activities.[8]

Dennett, indeed, has put forward the idea of our being composed of a whole hierarchy of homunculi which can be considered as more and more 'stupid' the lower their position in the hierarchy. But Dennett is an instrumentalist on these matters, so that, as far as he is concerned, this conception of things is to be considered only in terms of whether it is useful for the prediction of people's behaviour and not in terms of it having some psychological reality. Indeed one might think it difficult to consider matters in these terms except on this basis; we are not literally composed of homunculi, and many would think the reference to homunculi enough to justify rejection of the whole conception of things.

Realistically considered, sub-personal activities are on this view still, fundamentally, personal, although the person in question is not the person whose activities they were initially supposed to be. However, on any other conception the sub-personal activities and states could not be *anyone's* activities and states, and would not therefore be the activities or the kind of states that they were supposed to be – something that has to do with us but not at the personal level. We can engage in various activities, and sometimes, as we have seen, we can do so unconsciously, even when the activities are directed to the solution of an intellectual problem. It is totally another matter to suppose that we can engage in these activities sub-personally, and there is no justification, apart from what may be supposed to be a heuristic one, for the view that we are best and realistically viewed as a family or hierarchy of persons.[9]

I do not think, therefore, that the concept of the sub-personal as used in this way makes much sense. That does not mean that there is nothing that goes on in us below the level of the personal; it means that whatever does so go on is quite different from what is personal, and is not to be thought of in terms which have any analogy with the personal. Clearly much goes on at the physiological and physical level. It may be that the *function* of some or even much of what goes on in the brain is computational; that is to say that it may be that the brain functions to some extent as a computer. To that extent Marr's three levels can be preserved. But *we* do not function as computers, not even in part, let alone as a whole. It follows that there are limits to what can be derived from the invocation of the computational metaphor.

I believe too that reliance on that metaphor has tended to produce an over-simple view of the mind. That is not to say that the computational and other processes that may be involved in brain functioning are simple. It is clear that they are nothing of the kind. Rather it is that over-reliance on the computational metaphor produces too simple a conception of what a human being is even at the cognitive level. In particular, I hope that I have shown that we cannot regard the cognitive system as a black box such that the details of what goes on inside it can conceivably be made clear, supposing only that there is some form of input to it and some form of output from it.

In the end it is that background conception that encourages the over-simplicity. I have gone along with it to the extent that I have been concerned to make more clear what it should look like when we have a better and more realistic conception of what that input and output, properly speaking, are. But what emerges from that is that a better conception of perception and behaviour or action, which is what the input and output really come to, reveals that we cannot be concerned simply to gain a better view of what processes come between. For perception, for example, is not possible except in agents, and action is not simply what is causally brought about in the body by what goes on in between input and output. We need a much more complicated view of things than that.

I do not represent that merely as a vindication of folk psychology. It is common even among those defending folk psychology to represent it as summed up in the view that behaviour is to be explained in terms of complexes of beliefs and desires. I think that what is required is more complex and more subtle than that. People do not always do what they believe will satisfy a desire of theirs. Once we start on the road which leads from that, we inevitably broach complex patterns of understanding of people, which may be 'folk' in the sense that they are not technical, but which are extremely rich in their own way. Those who have claimed that folk psychology is poverty-stricken in its explanatory and predictive powers cannot have read any literature lately. One is tempted to say that they cannot have had much to do with other people.

That is not of course to say that the discipline of psychology cannot add to and sometimes correct that understanding. There are common stereotypes and prejudices which a more persistent examination of the facts can, and ought to, overcome. But there is nothing in what psychology can tell us which suggests that our common-sense understanding of ourselves and others is fundamentally at fault and should eventually, if not sooner, be discarded. Moreover, we are still a long way from understanding how psychological processes are to be related to their physical basis. All the theories offered at Marr level-2, as one might put it, do not really make that any the less true. That is not to say that they may not have some heuristic value and be suggestive in one direction or another. The faith that that is so is what promotes the study of artificial intelligence. But AI is not the whole, and perhaps not even a large part, of what is required for the proper study of man.

It would be nice to be able to offer advice to cognitive psychologists. That would, however, be presumptuous, and it might get in the way of discovery and enlightenment. For in science it is not always easy to predict what will come from what, and it is wrong for a philosopher to get in the way. But it is right for a philosopher to try to point to conceptual error and to present what may be a better system of concepts. It is right for anyone who has such insight to resist premature empire-building in the name of science, especially when the empire-building is motivated simply by what is the currently dominant ideology. And that is what I believe physicalism to be.

Notes

INTRODUCTION

1 F. C. Bartlett, *Remembering* (Cambridge University Press, Cambridge, 1932).

CHAPTER 1 BEHAVIOURISM

1 C. Taylor, *The Explanation of Behaviour* (Routledge & Kegan Paul, London, 1964), p. 143.
2 J. B. Watson, *Psychology from the Standpoint of a Behaviorist* (Lippincott, Philadelphia, 1919) and *Behaviorism* (Mouton, New York, 1925), especially the latter.
3 See e.g. Taylor, *The Explanation of Behaviour*, ch. 7, J. J. Gibson, *The Senses Considered as Perceptual Systems* (Houghton Mifflin, Boston, Mass., 1966 and Allen & Unwin, London, 1968), p. 28, and D. W. Hamlyn, 'Conditioning and behaviour', in *Explanation in the Behavioural Sciences*, ed. R. Borger and F. Cioffi (Cambridge University Press, Cambridge, 1970), pp. 139–52, also in D. W. Hamlyn, *Perception, Learning and the Self* (Routledge & Kegan Paul, London, 1983), pp. 91–106.
4 The idea was first introduced in a major way in B. F. Skinner, *The Behavior of Organisms* (Appleton-Century, New York, 1938).
5 See Hamlyn, 'Conditioning and behaviour'.
6 N. Malcolm, 'The conceivability of mechanism', *Philosophical Review*, 77 (1968), pp. 45–72.
7 This is a point which has wider implications for any theory that seeks to explain notions such as that of intention in terms of teleology in the non-purposive sense. That point will recur later.

CHAPTER 2   GOING INSIDE THE BLACK BOX

1   J. J. Gibson, *The Senses Considered as Perceptual Systems* (Houghton Mifflin, Boston, Mass., 1966 and Allen & Unwin, London, 1968).
2   For the details of this see D. W. Hamlyn, *The Psychology of Perception* (Routledge & Kegan Paul, London, 1957), ch. 4.
3   K. H. Pribram, 'Holonomy and structure in the organization of perception', in *Images, Perception and Knowledge*, ed. J. M. Nicholas (D. Reidel, Dordrecht, 1977), pp. 155–85; J. L. McClelland, D. E. Rumelhart and others, *Parallel Distributed Processing: Explorations in the Microstructure of Cognition* (2 vols, MIT Press, Cambridge, Mass., 1986).
4   Gibson, *The Senses Considered as Perceptual Systems*, p. 245.
5   See e.g. p. 40.
6   F. Dretske, *Knowledge and the Flow of Information* (Basil Blackwell, Oxford, 1983).
7   Particularly in F. Dretske, 'Misrepresentation', in *Belief: Form, Content and Function*, ed. R. J. Bogdan (Clarendon Press, Oxford, 1986), pp. 17–36.
8   For a recent discussion of these issues, see R. J. Bogdan, 'Information and semantic cognition: an ontological account', *Mind and Language*, 3 (1988), pp. 81–122. The number of the journal also contains commentaries by David J. Israel and Fred Dretske, with a reply by Bogdan.
9   Cf. my 'Conditioning and behaviour' and some of the other papers in D. W. Hamlyn, *Perception, Learning and the Self* (Routledge & Kegan Paul, London, 1983).
10 See also on this C. Peacocke, *Thoughts: An Essay on Content* (Basil Blackwell, Oxford, 1986), pt IV.
11 Cf. A. P. Griffiths, 'On belief', *Proc. Arist. Soc.*, 63 (1962/3), pp. 167–87, reprinted in *Knowledge and Belief*, ed. A. P. Griffiths (Oxford University Press, Oxford, 1967), pp. 127–43.
12 J. Fodor, *The Modularity of Mind* (Bradford Books, MIT Press, Cambridge, Mass., 1983).
13 An analogous account of some of this, particularly what is said about transducers and the processes which then operate on the results of their operation, is to be found in Z. W. Pylyshyn, *Computation and Cognition* (Bradford Books, MIT Press, Cambridge, Mass., 1984), esp. ch. 6.
14 On this point see e.g. J. Russell, *Explaining Mental Life* (Macmillan, London and Basingstoke, 1984), esp. ch. 1.

CHAPTER 3   INSIDE THE BLACK BOX

1   Pierre Duhem lived from 1861 to 1916. The best account of his philosophy of science is to be found in his *The Aim and Structure of Physical Theory*, trans. P. P. Wiener (Princeton University Press, Princeton, NJ, 1954).
2   D. Dennett, *Brainstorms* (Bradford Books, MIT Press, Cambridge, Mass., 1978 and Harvester, Brighton, 1978). See also his 'Three kinds of intentional psychology', in *Reduction, Time and Reality*, ed. R. Healey (Cambridge University Press, Cambridge, 1981), pp. 37–61, and his more recent *The Intentional Stance* (Bradford Books, MIT Press, Cambridge, Mass., 1987).
3   J. Fodor, 'Fodor's guide to mental representation', *Mind*, 94 (1985), pp. 76–100.
4   B. A. Farrell, 'Experience', *Mind*, 59 (1950), pp. 170–98, also in *Philosophy of Mind*, ed. V. Chappell (Prentice-Hall, Englewood Cliffs, NJ, 1962), pp. 23–48; R. Rorty, 'Mind–body identity, privacy and categories', *Review of Metaphysics*, 19 (1965), pp. 25–54, also in *The Philosophy of Mind*, ed. S. N. Hampshire (Harper & Row, New York, 1966) (see also his *Philosophy and the Mirror of Nature*, Basil Blackwell, Oxford, 1980); Paul M. Churchland, *Matter and Consciousness* (Bradford Books, MIT Press, Cambridge, Mass., 1984), and 'Eliminative materialism and the propositional attitudes', *Journal of Philosophy*, 78 (1981), pp. 67–90; Patricia S. Churchland, 'A perspective on mind–brain research', *J. Phil.*, 77 (1980), pp. 185–207.
5   There is now a considerable literature on this. A brief account of some of it is to be found in D. W. Hamlyn, *Metaphysics* (Cambridge University Press, Cambridge, 1984), ch. 8.
6   See e.g. S. P. Stich, *From Folk Psychology to Cognitive Science* (Bradford Books, MIT Press, Cambridge, Mass., 1983), who makes great use of the notion of sub-doxastic states.
7   There is again a brief discussion of this issue, with some references to the literature in Hamlyn, *Metaphysics*, ch. 8.
8   For references see Fodor, 'Fodor's guide to mental representation'.
9   There is a particularly graphic discussion of this point with respect to memory in N. Malcolm, *Memory and Mind* (Cornell University Press, Ithaca, NY, 1977).
10   John Heil has, in his 'Does cognitive psychology rest on a mistake?', *Mind*, 90 (1981), pp. 321–42, argued that for something to count as a representation it must be used as such. This is probably too strict. See also J. Heil, *Perception and Cognition* (University of

158 NOTES

California Press, Berkeley, Los Angeles and London, 1983).

11 It is because something may have a representational function without necessarily being designed as such that I expressed reservations about John Heil's thesis in the previous note.

12 See S. M. Kosslyn, *Image and Mind* (Harvard University Press, Cambridge, Mass., 1980); Z. W. Pylyshyn, *Computation and Cognition* (Bradford Books, MIT Press, Cambridge, Mass., 1984), ch. 8, plus the other references to papers by him given there; A. V. Paavio, 'Images, propositions and knowledge', in *Images, Perception and Knowledge*, ed. J. M. Nicholas (D. Reidel, Dordrecht, 1977), pp. 47–71. See also J. Russell, *Explaining Mental Life* (Macmillan, London and Basingstoke, 1984), ch. 6, and U. Neisser, *Cognition and Reality* (W. H. Freeman, San Francisco, 1976), ch. 7.

13 D. Marr, *Vision* (W. H. Freeman, San Francisco, 1982), p. 20. It is only fair to add that his tragically early death may have prevented further clarification of what he has to say.

14 Daniel C. Dennett, 'Styles of mental representation', *Proc. Arist. Soc.*, 83 (1982/3), pp. 213–26.

15 See Fodor, 'Fodor's guide to mental representation', and also his paper 'Propositional attitudes', *The Monist*, 61 (1978), pp. 501–23, which is included in J. Fodor, *Representations* (Bradford Books, MIT Press, Cambridge, Mass., 1980 and Harvester, Brighton, 1981), pp. 177–203. More recent discussions by him are to be found in J. Fodor, *Psychosemantics* (Bradford Books, MIT Press, Cambridge, Mass., 1987). A similar argument is to be found in Pylyshyn, *Computation and Cognition*, pp. 24ff.

16 H. Field, 'Mental representation', *Erkenntnis*, 13 (1978), pp. 9–61; also in *Readings in Philosophy of Psychology*, vol. 2, ed. N. Block, (Harvard University Press, Cambridge, Mass., 1981).

17 B. Russell, *Problems of Philosophy* (Oxford University Press, London and Oxford, 1912), ch. 12.

18 B. Russell, 'The philosophy of logical atomism', reprinted from *The Monist*, 1918–19 in *Logic and Knowledge*, ed. R. C. Marsh (Allen & Unwin, London, 1956).

19 G. Frege, 'On sense and reference', in *Translations*, ed. P. Geach and M. Black (Basil Blackwell, Oxford, 1952).

20 See J. Fodor, *The Language of Thought* (Crowell, New York, 1975 and Harvester, Brighton, 1975). Dennett's criticism is to be found in a critical notice of that book in *Mind*, 86 (1977), pp. 265–80, also in D. Dennett, *Brainstorms* (Bradford Books, MIT Press, Cambridge, Mass., 1978 and Harvester, Brighton, 1978).

21 Plato, *Theaetetus* 189e and *Sophist* 263e.

22 In *Behavioral and Brain Sciences*, 3 (1980), pp. 63–73; also in his *Representations*, pp. 225–53.

23 The paper was originally given as a lecture in Cincinatti.

24 See also J. Fodor, 'Individualism and supervenience', *Proc. Arist. Soc., Supp. Vol.*, 60 (1986), with the reply by Martin Davies, pp. 263–83.

25 H. Putnam, 'The meaning of "meaning"', in his *Mind, Language and Reality: Philosophical Papers*, vol. 2 (Cambridge University Press, Cambridge, 1975), pp. 215–71.

26 T. Burge, 'Individualism and the mental', *Midwest Studies in Philosophy*, 4 (1979), pp. 73–121, and 'Other bodies', in *Thought and Object*, ed. A. Woodfield (Clarendon Press, Oxford, 1982), pp. 97–120.

27 See e.g. D. W. Hamlyn, 'Cognitive systems, "folk psychology", and knowledge', *Cognition*, 10 (1981), pp. 115–18.

28 Stich, *From Folk Psychology to Cognitive Science*. See also his 'Autonomous psychology and the belief–desire thesis', *The Monist*, 61 (1978), pp. 573–91.

29 See e.g. W. V. Quine, 'Two dogmas of empiricism', in his *From a Logical Point of View* (Harvard University Press, Cambridge, Mass., 1953), and many other writings of his.

30 See several of the papers in D. Davidson, *Essays on Actions and Events* (Clarendon Press, Oxford, 1980).

31 For an analogous argument put in terms of what is involved in concept possession, see my 'What exactly is social about the origins of understanding?', in D. W. Hamlyn, *Perception, Learning and the Self* (Routledge & Kegan Paul, London, 1983).

32 It is possible to argue that all these points suggest a model for the understanding of the brain-processes which underlie beliefs and knowledge which is quite opposed to any that seeks to decompose the processes involved into discrete elements which are then combined into complexes. There has emerged recently a different, connectionist, model, which presupposes degrees in the strength of connections between parts of the system and degrees in the extent to which there is activation at nodes in the system. This is the theory of parallel distributed processing referred to in an earlier chapter. See e.g. J. L. McClelland, D. E. Rumelhart and others, *Parallel Distributed Processing: Explorations in the Microstructure of Cognition* (2 vols, MIT Press, Cambridge, Mass., 1986).

33 See e.g. G. Ryle, *The Concept of Mind* (Hutchinson, London, 1949), ch. 5.

34 See e.g. D. M. Armstrong, *Belief, Truth and Knowledge* (Cambridge University Press, Cambridge, 1973).

CHAPTER 4   PERCEPTION I: A PROPER VIEW OF INPUT?

1 See D. W. Hamlyn, *Sensation and Perception* (Routledge & Kegan Paul, London, 1961).
2 See again Hamlyn, *Sensation and Perception*, ch. 9.
3 J. J. Gibson, *The Perception of the Visual World* (Houghton Mifflin, Boston, Mass., 1950).
4 J. J. Gibson, *The Senses Considered as Perceptual Systems* (Houghton Mifflin, Boston, Mass., 1966 and Allen & Unwin, London, 1968).
5 See Gibson, *Senses*, p. 245. Fred Dretske argues otherwise in his *Knowledge and the Flow of Information* (Basil Blackwell, Oxford, 1983), pp. 255–6, but Gibson's remarks on p. 245 of his book are unequivocal.
6 There have been criticisms of Gibson on this point from many different sources, but see, for example, my own 'The concept of information in Gibson's theory of perception', *Journal for the Theory of Social Behaviour*, 7 (1977), pp. 5–16, also in D. W. Hamlyn, *Perception, Learning and the Self* (Routledge & Kegan Paul, London, 1983), pp. 30–42. There is also similar material in my 'Perception, information and attention' in the same volume, pp. 57–68.
7 J. J. Gibson, *The Ecological Approach to Visual Perception* (Houghton Mifflin, Boston, Mass., 1979).
8 See e.g. G. W. Humphreys and M. J. Riddoch, *To See But Not To See* (Erlbaum, London, 1987).
9 See for example R. Gregory, 'Choosing a paradigm for perception', in *Handbook of Perception*, ed. E. C. Carterette and M. F. Friedman, vol. 1 (Academic Press, New York and London, 1974), pp. 255–83.
10 U. Neisser, *Cognition and Reality* (W. H. Freeman, San Francisco, 1976), ch. 2.
11 See also J. S. Bruner, *Beyond the Information Given*, ed. J. M. Anglin, (Allen & Unwin, London, 1974).
12 D. Marr, *Vision* (W. H. Freeman, San Francisco, 1982).
13 Neisser is obviously one example of this. See also the papers by P. A. Manfredi, and G. W. Humphreys and M. J. Riddoch in *Mind and Language*, 1 (1986), pp. 181–200 and 201–12, with the references given by them.
14 See my 'Perception and agency', in Hamlyn, *Perception, Learning and the Self*, pp. 43–56, esp. pp. 47–8. As I shall suggest in the next

chapter, one of the things on which Marr puts great emphasis – the fact that random-dot stereograms can produce experiences as of depth – shows something about the effect on experience of what are features of two-dimensional surfaces; but to have an experience as of depth is not as yet to perceive things as three-dimensional.

15 Apart from Marr's *Vision*, there is a useful account of these matters in D. Marr and H. K. Nishihara, 'Visual information processing: artificial intelligence and the sensorium of sight', *Technology Review*, October 1978, pp. 28–49.

16 There is some similarity between this and the theory of perception advocated by Schopenhauer, except that the latter inevitably thought that the *a priori* knowledge presupposed in perception was conscious knowledge. See D. W. Hamlyn, *Schopenhauer* (Routledge & Kegan Paul, London, 1980), pp. 19–21, where I present a rather pessimistic critique of Schopenhauer's theory. For Marr, grounds for believing in such *a priori* constraints are provided by the fact that the random-dot stereograms referred to in note 14 produce of themselves an impression of depth. Since the dot-patterns are random, it is taken that the impression of depth must be a function purely of the workings of the perceptual mechanisms.

17 There is perhaps a certain similarity between this way of thinking of our conception of *the* shape of objects and the account offered by the Gestaltist Kurt Koffka of what we take to be *the* shape or *the* size of an object. See D. W. Hamlyn, *The Psychology of Perception* (Routledge & Kegan Paul, London, 1957), pp. 68–70.

18 I have in the past made similar criticisms of Gibson. See Hamlyn, *The Psychology of Perception*, ch. 5, and my 'The concept of information in Gibson's theory of perception', in Hamlyn, *Perception, Learning and the Self*, pp. 30–42.

CHAPTER 5   PERCEPTION II: WHAT IS PERCEPTION?

1 See T. Reid, *Essays on the Intellectual Powers of Man*, ed. A. D. Woozley (Macmillan, London and Basingstoke, 1941). There is a section on Reid, as well as a general discussion of the concepts of sensation and perception, in D. W. Hamlyn, *Sensation and Perception* (Routledge & Kegan Paul, London, 1961). See also D. W. Hamlyn, *Experience and the Growth of Understanding* (Routledge & Kegan Paul, London, 1978), ch. 5.

2 See my 'Unconscious inference and judgment in perception' and

'Perception, information and attention', in D. W. Hamlyn, *Perception, Learning and the Self* (Routledge & Kegan Paul, London, 1983), pp. 11–29 and 57–68.

3 G. Ryle, *The Concept of Mind* (Hutchinson, London, 1949), pp. 240ff. and his 'Sensation', in *Contemporary British Philosophy, 3rd Series*, ed. H. D. Lewis (Allen & Unwin, London, 1956), pp. 427–43.

4 C. Peacocke, *Sense and Content* (Clarendon Press, Oxford, 1983), ch. 1.

5 See e.g. L. Weiskrantz, 'Trying to bridge the neuropsychological gap between monkey and man', *British Journal of Psychology*, 68 (1977), pp. 431–45, and L. Weiskrantz and others, 'Visual capacity in the hemianopic field following a restricted ablation', *Brain*, 97 (1974), pp. 709–28. I have had a few words to say about the phenomenon in my 'Perception, information and attention', in Hamlyn, *Perception, Learning and the Self*, pp. 57–68, esp. p. 59.

6 See J. J. Gibson, *The Senses Considered as Perceptual Systems* (Houghton Mifflin, Boston, Mass., 1966 and Allen & Unwin, London, 1968), p. 2, and my discussion of these issues in my 'The concept of information in Gibson's theory of perception', in Hamlyn, *Perception, Learning and the Self*, pp. 30–42.

7 See e.g. M. Von Senden, *Space and Sight*, trans. P. Heath (Methuen, London, 1960). This affects the question of the possible solutions to 'Molyneux's problem' (the question that Molyneux put to Locke in the eighteenth century, as to whether a congenitally blind person would, on having his sight restored, be able to perceive the properties of things which he had previously perceived by touch). See M. J. Morgan, *Molyneux's Question* (Cambridge University Press, Cambridge, 1977), and D. W. Hamlyn, *The Psychology of Perception* (Routledge & Kegan Paul, London, 1957), pp. 96–7.

8 See I. Rock, *The Nature of Perceptual Adaptation* (Basic Books Inc., New York and London, 1966). For an interesting discussion of the notion of 'looks' see A. Millar, 'What's in a look?', *Proc. Arist. Soc.*, 86 (1985/6), pp. 83–97.

9 See e.g. the report of this and the further references given, including an account of the experience by a blind philosophy student, by John Heil, *Perception and Cognition* (University of California Press, Berkeley, Los Angeles and London, 1983), pp. 15ff. and 74ff. He also has things to say about 'blind sight'.

10 See F. H. Bradley, 'In what sense are psychical states extended?', in his *Collected Papers* (2 vols, Clarendon Press, Oxford, 1935), vol. 2,

pp. 349ff. Bradley was reacting to James Ward, who spoke of the 'extensity' of sensations. See also Hamlyn, *Sensation and Perception*, pp. 160–2, and, for more detail, D. W. Hamlyn, 'Bradley, Ward and Stout', in *Historical Roots of Contemporary Psychology*, ed. B. B. Wolman, (Harper & Row, New York, 1968), pp. 298–320.

11 See D. W. Hamlyn, 'The visual field and perception', *Proc. Arist. Soc., Supp. Vol.*, 31 (1957), pp. 107–24.

12 See also R. V. Scruton, *Art and Imagination* (Methuen, London, 1974), pt 2.

13 It may be again worth noting in passing that this fact is arguably more consistent with the connectionism involved in parallel distributed processing as a model for the neurological underpinning of cognitive processes than it is with any theory that makes the having of a concept an all or none matter, as a theory presupposing representations seems to do.

14 See on this P. F. Strawson, 'Imagination and perception', in his *Freedom and Resentment* (Methuen, London, 1974), pp. 45–65. See too my 'Unconscious inference and judgment in perception', in Hamlyn, *Perception, Learning and the Self*, pp. 11–29, esp. pp. 22–3.

15 See e.g. D. M. Armstrong, *Perception and the Physical World* (Routledge & Kegan Paul, London, 1961) and *The Materialist Theory of the Mind* (Routledge & Kegan Paul, London, 1968), and G. Pitcher, *A Theory of Perception* (Princeton University Press, Princeton, NJ, 1971).

16 F. Dretske, *Seeing and Knowing* (Routledge & Kegan Paul, London, 1969).

17 T. G. R. Bower, *Development in Infancy* (W. H. Freeman, San Francisco, 1974). See also J. Russell, *The Acquisition of Knowledge* (Macmillan, London and Basingstoke, 1978) and his 'Reasons for retaining the view that there is perceptual development in childhood', in *Philosophical Perspectives on Developmental Psychology* ed. J. Russell (Basil Blackwell, Oxford, 1987), pp. 81–115.

18 N. Malcolm, *Memory and Mind* (Cornell University Press, Ithaca, NY, 1977) rightly insists on this kind of point. It is of a part with Wittgenstein's criticisms in his *Philosophical Investigations* (Basil Blackwell, Oxford, 1953) of the 'myth of the mental process' – the supposition that whenever we invoke a mental concept we are making reference to, or at least presuppose the existence of, some process which could equally have its parallel in neurological or other physical terms. This is not to say, note, that there are mental

states which have no physical basis; it is to cast a sceptical eye on the claim that the concepts in question all pick out mental states or processes.

19 I have in mind, for example, the work of A. M. Treisman. See e.g. her 'Strategies and models of selective attention', *Psychological Review*, 76 (1969), pp. 282–99. There is some discussion of this work in U. Neisser, *Cognition and Reality* (W. H. Freeman, San Francisco, 1976), ch. 5. Neisser quite rightly connects the notion of attention with that of consciousness.

20 See on this e.g. R. Gregory, *Eye and Brain* (Weidenfeld & Nicolson, London, 1966), ch. 7.

21 I have argued this in my 'Perception and agency', in Hamlyn, *Perception, Learning and the Self*, pp. 43–56, and much of what follows here is derived from that source.

22 R. Held and A. Hein, 'Movement-produced stimulation in the development of visually guided behavior', *Journal of Comparative Physiology*, 56 (1963), pp. 872–6.

23 Michotte's experiments designed to show something about our perception of causality and substancehood, interesting though they are if taken as phenomenology, really fall foul of that objection. See A. Michotte, *La perception de la causalité*, 2nd ed, 1954 and *Causalité, permanence et réalité phénoménales*, 1962 (both Publications Universitaires de Louvain, Louvain).

24 J. S. Bruner, *Beyond the Information Given*, ed. J. M. Anglin (Allen & Unwin, London, 1974), p. 323.

25 See J. Hopkins, 'Synthesis in the imagination, psychoanalysis, infantile experience and the concept of an object', in *Philosophical Perspectives on Developmental Psychology*, ed. Russell, pp. 140–72.

26 See some of the papers on this in *Readings in the Philosophy of Psychology*, ed. N. Block (Harvard University Press, Cambridge, Mass., 1980), vol. 1. For a brief account of the issues see D. W. Hamlyn, *Metaphysics* (Cambridge University Press, Cambridge, 1984), pp. 183–5.

CHAPTER 6   THE EFFECT OF THE PAST

1 See e.g. N. Chomsky, *Language and Mind* (Hartcourt Brace, New York, 1968), p. 74. It is only fair to add that Chomsky's views have undergone modifications in many subsequent writings.

2 M. Polanyi, *Personal Knowledge* (University of Chicago Press,

Chicago, 1958), and *The Tacit Dimension* (Doubleday, New York, 1966).

3   See e.g. J. Fodor, 'The appeal to tacit knowledge in psychological explanation', *J. Phil.*, 65 (1968), pp. 627–40, and Z. W. Pylyshyn, *Computation and Cognition* (Bradford Books, MIT Press, Cambridge, Mass., 1984), ch. 8.

4   See my 'What exactly is social about the origins of understanding?', in *Social Cognition*, ed. G. Butterworth and P. Light (Harvester, Brighton, 1982), pp. 17–31, also in D. W. Hamlyn, *Perception, Learning and the Self* (Routledge & Kegan Paul, London, 1983), pp. 162–77. See also D. W. Hamlyn, *Experience and the Growth of Understanding* (Routledge & Kegan Paul, London, 1978), esp. chs 6 and 7.

5   See Hamlyn, *Experience and the Growth of Understanding*, ch. 2.

6   See J. Fodor, 'The present status of the innateness controversy', in J. Fodor, *Representations* (Bradford Books, MIT Press, Cambridge, Mass., 1980 and Harvester, Brighton, 1981), ch. 10. See also Fodor's contribution to *Language and Learning: The Debate between Jean Piaget and Noam Chomsky*, ed. M. Piatelli-Palmarini (Routledge & Kegan Paul, London, 1980).

7   The problem involved is also very similar to that underlying Piaget's worries about how new knowledge is possible in biological terms.

8   A. Woodfield, 'On the very idea of acquiring a concept', in *Philosophical Perspectives on Developmental Psychology*, ed. J. Russell (Basil Blackwell, London, 1987), pp. 17–30, esp. pp. 26–7.

9   For similar considerations see my 'What exactly is social about the origins of understanding?'. That paper, as its title makes clear, also raises the issue of the social conditions of conceptual understanding.

10   It is important to note all the 'ifs' in the above account of the geese. The same would apply to other animals. I say only that *if* certain things are so then other things must be so. I do not wish to practise *a priori* zoology.

11   See K. Popper, *Objective Knowledge* (Clarendon Press, Oxford, 1972).

12   See Hamlyn, 'What exactly is social about the origins of understanding?'. The argument is also to be found in D. W. Hamlyn, 'The concept of social reality', in *Explaining Social Behavior*, ed. P. Secord (Sage Publications, Beverly Hills, London and New Delhi, 1982), pp. 189–209. I give only an abbreviated version of the argument here.

13   See further on this D. W. Hamlyn, 'Reply to David E. Cooper', *J. of Phil. of Education*, 14 (1980), pp. 105–8.

14 See the argument in D. W. Hamlyn, 'Human learning', in *Philosophy of Psychology*, ed. S. C. Brown (Macmillan, London and Basingstoke, 1974), pp. 139–57; also in Hamlyn, *Perception, Learning and the Self*, pp. 132–48, esp. pp. 143–4.

CHAPTER 7 OUTPUT

1 D. Davidson, 'Actions, reasons and causes', *J. Phil.*, 60 (1963), pp. 685–700; reprinted in his *Essays on Actions and Events* (Clarendon Press, Oxford, 1980), pp. 3–19.

2 J. Hornsby, *Actions* (Routledge & Kegan Paul, London, 1980), esp. ch. 1. I myself hinted at such a distinction in D. W. Hamlyn, 'Behaviour', *Philosophy*, 28 (1953), pp. 132–45, also in *Philosophy of Mind*, ed. V. Chappell (Prentice-Hall, Englewood Cliffs, NJ, 1962), pp. 60–73.

3 D. Davidson, 'Freedom to act', originally in *Essays on Freedom of Action*, ed. T. Honderich (Routledge & Kegan Paul, London, 1973), but reprinted in Davidson's *Essays on Actions and Events*, pp. 63–81.

4 See e.g. C. Peacocke, *Holistic Explanation: Action, Space, Interpretation* (Clarendon Press, Oxford, 1979).

5 See further on this D. W. Hamlyn, 'Schopenhauer on action and the will', in *Idealism: Past and Present*, ed. G. N. A. Vesey (Cambridge University Press, Cambridge, 1982), pp. 127–40, esp. pp. 137–8. I believe that Schopenhauer had a surer insight here.

6 This is a comment on another paper in that book, 'Intending', written in 1978. The views of G. E. M. Anscombe which are referred to are to be found in her book *Intention* (Basil Blackwell, Oxford, 1957).

7 There is an interesting discussion of this point in N. Fleming, 'Autonomy of the will', *Mind*, 90 (1981), pp. 201–23. Fleming uses the example of Krishna's advice to Arjuna before the battle at the beginning of the *Bhagavad Gita*.

8 See S. N. Hampshire, *Thought and Action* (Chatto & Windus, London, 1959) for the idea of practical knowledge, and Anscombe, *Intention* for that of knowledge without observation.

9 B. O'Shaughnessy, *The Will* (2 vols, Cambridge University Press, Cambridge, 1980), vol. 2, ch. 10.

10 See my papers 'Unconscious intentions' and 'Self-deception', included in D. W. Hamlyn, *Perception, Learning and the Self* (Rout-

ledge & Kegan Paul, London, 1983), pp. 181–93 and 194–207. It may be worth noting that such 'unconscious knowledge' is not the tacit knowledge which was discussed in the previous chapter; it is plain ordinary knowledge.

11 See D. W. Hamlyn, *Schopenhauer* (Routledge & Kegan Paul, London, 1980), ch. 5, esp. p. 85.

12 For more on this point see D. W. Hamlyn, 'Motivation', in *Education, Values and Mind, Essays for R. S. Peters*, ed. D. E. Cooper (Routledge & Kegan Paul, London, 1986), pp. 188–200.

CHAPTER 8   CONCLUSION

1 A recent example is L. R. Baker, *Saving Belief* (Princeton University Press, Princeton, NJ, 1987).

2 See e.g. C. Peacocke, *Thoughts: An Essay on Content* (Basil Blackwell, Oxford, 1986), pt IV, p. 138.

3 Particularly in my 'What exactly is social about the origins of understanding?', in D. W. Hamlyn, *Perception, Learning and the Self* (Routledge & Kegan Paul, London, 1983), pp. 162–77. As the title of the paper indicates, I was there concerned with this in relation to the question how knowledge and understanding can come about in the individual at all, but the point is a quite general one.

4 It may be worth pointing out again that this does *not* reduce all psychology, and cognitive psychology in particular, to social psychology, since, whatever the framework of ideas presupposed, the questions asked by cognitive and social psychologists are different.

5 See J. Hadamard, *The Psychology of Invention in the Mathematical Field* (Princeton University Press, Princeton, NJ, 1945), who also quotes Poincaré.

6 See D. W. Hamlyn, 'Thinking', in *Contemporary British Philosophy, 4th Series*, ed. H. D. Lewis (Allen & Unwin, London, 1976), pp. 100–12.

7 Cf. Kant's famous remark in his *Critique of Pure Reason*, B131, that 'it must be possible for the "I think" to accompany all my representations'. This indeed insists on something even more stringent than what I have been concerned with so far – that anything engaging in something that has to do with representations must be able to be self-conscious, not merely conscious of what it is engaging in. Nevertheless, the word 'possible' is important in Kant's formulation; he is not insisting that every personal activity be conscious.

8 See D. Dennett, 'Intentional systems' and various other writings in his *Brainstorms* (Bradford Books, MIT Press, Cambridge, Mass., 1978 and Harvester, Brighton, 1978) and elsewhere.

9 There may be other phenomena, including those involved in cases of split personality, which may seem to give some credence to that idea. But it should be noted (a) that these are very different phenomena from those with which we are at present concerned, and (b) split personality does not necessarily entail split *persons*.

Bibliography

Anscombe, G. E. M., *Intention* (Basil Blackwell, Oxford, 1957).

Armstrong, D. M., *Perception and the Physical World* (Routledge & Kegan Paul, London, 1961).

Armstrong, D. M., *The Materialist Theory of the Mind* (Routledge & Kegan Paul, London, 1968).

Armstrong, D. M., *Belief, Truth and Knowledge* (Cambridge University Press, Cambridge, 1973).

Baker, L. R., *Saving Belief* (Princeton University Press, Princeton, NJ, 1987).

Bartlett, F. C., *Remembering* (Cambridge University Press, Cambridge, 1932).

Block, N. (ed.), *Readings in Philosophy of Psychology* (2 vols, Harvard University Press, Cambridge, Mass., vol. 1 1980, vol. 2 1981).

Bogdan, R. J., 'Information and semantic cognition: an ontological account', *Mind and Language*, 3 (1988), pp. 81–122.

Bower, T. G. R., *Development in Infancy* (W. H. Freeman, San Francisco, 1974).

Bradley, F. H., 'In what sense are psychical states extended?', in his *Collected Papers* (Clarendon Press, Oxford, 1935), vol. 2, pp. 349ff.

Bruner, J. S., *Beyond the Information Given*, ed. J. M. Anglin (Allen & Unwin, London, 1974).

Burge, T., 'Individualism and the mental', *Midwest Studies in Philosophy*, 4 (1979), pp. 73–121.

Burge, T., 'Other bodies', in *Thought and Object*, ed. A. Woodfield (Clarendon Press, Oxford, 1982), pp. 97–120.

Chappell, V. (ed.), *Philosophy of Mind* (Prentice-Hall, Englewood Cliffs, NJ, 1962).

Chomsky, N., *Language and Mind* (Hartcourt Brace, New York, 1968).

Churchland, Patricia S., 'A perspective on mind–brain research', *Journal of Philosophy*, 77 (1980), pp. 185–207.

Churchland, Paul M., 'Eliminative materialism and the propositional attitudes', *Journal of Philosophy*, 78 (1981), pp. 67–90.

Churchland, Paul M., *Matter and Consciousness* (Bradford Books, MIT Press, Cambridge, Mass., 1984).

Davidson, D., 'Actions, reasons and causes', *Journal of Philosophy*, 60 (1963), pp. 685–700, also in *Essays on Actions and Events*, pp. 3–19.

Davidson, D., 'Freedom to act', in *Essays on Freedom of Action*, ed. T. Honderich (Routledge & Kegan Paul, London, 1973), also in *Essays on Actions and Events*, pp. 63–81.

Davidson, D., 'Intending' (1978), in *Essays on Actions and Events*, pp. 83–102.

Davidson, D., *Essays on Actions and Events* (Clarendon Press, Oxford, 1980).

Dennett, D., *Brainstorms* (Bradford Books, MIT Press, Cambridge, Mass., 1978 and Harvester, Brighton, 1978).

Dennett, D., 'Three kinds of intentional psychology', in *Reduction, Time and Reality*, ed. R. Healey (Cambridge University Press, Cambridge, 1981), pp. 37–61.

Dennett, D., 'Styles of mental representation', *Proceedings of the Aristotelian Society*, 83 (1982/3), pp. 213–26.

Dennett, D., *The Intentional Stance* (Bradford Books, MIT Press, Cambridge, Mass., 1987).

Dretske, F., *Seeing and Knowing* (Routledge & Kegan Paul, London, 1969).

Dretske, F., *Knowledge and the Flow of Information* (Basil Blackwell, Oxford, 1983).

Dretske, F., 'Misrepresentation', in *Belief: Form, Content and Function*, ed. R. J. Bogdan (Clarendon Press, Oxford, 1986), pp. 17–36.

Duhem, P., *The Aim and Structure of Physical Theory*, trans. P. P. Wiener (Princeton University Press, Princeton, NJ, 1954).

Farrell, B. A., 'Experience', *Mind*, 59 (1950), pp. 170–98, also in *Philosophy of Mind*, ed. V. Chappell, pp. 23–48.

Field, H., 'Mental representation', *Erkenntnis*, 13 (1978), pp. 9–61, also in *Readings in Philosophy of Psychology*, vol. 2, ed. N. Block, pp. 78–114.

Fleming, N., 'Autonomy of the will', *Mind*, 90 (1981), pp. 201–23.

Fodor, J., 'The appeal to tacit knowledge in psychological explanation', *Journal of Philosophy*, 65 (1968), pp. 627–40.

Fodor, J., *The Language of Thought* (Crowell, New York, 1975 and Harvester, Brighton, 1975).

Fodor, J., 'Propositional attitudes', *The Monist*, 61 (1978), pp. 501–23, also in *Representations*, pp. 177–203.

Fodor, J., 'Methodological solipsism considered as a research strategy for cognitive psychology', *Behavioral and Brain Sciences*, 3 (1980), pp. 63–73, also in *Representations*, pp. 225–53.

Fodor, J., 'The present status of the innateness controversy' (1980), in *Representations*, pp. 257–316.

Fodor, J., *Representations* (Bradford Books, MIT Press, Cambridge, Mass., 1980 and Harvester, Brighton, 1981).

Fodor, J., *The Modularity of Mind* (Bradford Books, MIT Press, Cambridge, Mass., 1983).

Fodor, J., 'Fodor's guide to mental representation', *Mind*, 94 (1985), pp. 76–100.

Fodor, J., 'Individualism and supervenience', *Proceedings of the Aristotelian Society, Supp. Vol.*, 60 (1986), with a reply by Martin Davies, pp. 263–83.

Fodor, J., *Psychosemantics* (Bradford Books, MIT Press, Cambridge, Mass., 1987).

Frege, G., 'On sense and reference', in *Translations*, ed. P. Geach and M. Black (Basil Blackwell, Oxford, 1952).

Gibson, J. J., *The Perception of the Visual World* (Houghton Mifflin, Boston, Mass., 1950).

Gibson, J. J., *The Senses Considered as Perceptual Systems* (Houghton Mifflin, Boston, Mass., 1966 and Allen & Unwin, London, 1968).

Gibson, J. J., *The Ecological Approach to Visual Perception* (Houghton Mifflin, Boston, Mass., 1979).

Gregory, R., *Eye and Brain* (Weidenfeld & Nicolson, London, 1966).

Gregory, R., 'Choosing a paradigm for perception', in *Handbook of Perception*, ed. E. C. Carterette and M. F. Friedman, vol. 1 (Academic Press, New York and London, 1974), pp. 255–83.

Griffiths, A. P., 'On belief', *Proceedings of the Aristotelian Society*, 63 (1962/3), pp. 167–87, also in *Knowledge and Belief*, ed. A. P. Griffiths (Oxford University Press, Oxford, 1967), pp. 127–43.

Hadamard, J., *The Psychology of Invention in the Mathematical Field* (Princeton University Press, Princeton, NJ, 1945).

Hamlyn, D. W., 'Behaviour', *Philosophy*, 28 (1953), pp. 132–45, also in *Philosophy of Mind*, ed. V. Chappell, pp. 60–73.

Hamlyn, D. W., *The Psychology of Perception* (Routledge & Kegan Paul, London, 1957).

Hamlyn, D. W., 'The visual field and perception', *Proceedings of the Aristotelian Society, Supp. Vol.*, 31 (1957), pp. 107–24.

Hamlyn, D. W., *Sensation and Perception* (Routledge & Kegan Paul, London, 1961).

Hamlyn, D. W., 'Bradley, Ward and Stout', in *Historical Roots of Contemporary Psychology*, ed. B. B. Wolman (Harper & Row, New York and London, 1968), pp. 298–320.

Hamlyn, D. W., 'Conditioning and behaviour', in *Explanation in the Behavioural Sciences*, ed. R. Borger and F. Cioffi (Cambridge University Press, Cambridge, 1970), pp. 139–52, also in *Perception, Learning and the Self*, pp. 91–106.

Hamlyn, D. W., 'Human learning', in *Philosophy of Psychology*, ed. S. C. Brown (Macmillan, London and Basingstoke, 1974), pp. 139–57, also in *Philosophy of Education*, ed. R. S. Peters (Oxford University Press, London, 1973), pp. 178–94, and *Perception, Learning and the Self*, pp. 132–48.

Hamlyn, D. W., 'Unconscious inference and judgment in perception' (1974), in *Images, Perception and Knowledge*, ed. J. M. Nicholas, pp. 195–212, also in *Perception, Learning and the Self*, pp. 11–29.

Hamlyn, D. W., 'Thinking', in *Contemporary British Philosophy, 4th Series*, ed. H. D. Lewis (Allen & Unwin, London, 1976), pp. 100–12.

Hamlyn, D. W., 'The concept of information in Gibson's theory of perception', *Journal for the Theory of Social Behaviour*, 7 (1977), pp. 5–16, also in *Perception, Learning and the Self*, pp. 30–42.

Hamlyn, D. W., *Experience and the Growth of Understanding* (Routledge & Kegan Paul, London, 1978).

Hamlyn, D. W., 'Perception and agency', *The Monist*, 61 (1978), pp. 536–47, also in *Perception, Learning and the Self*, pp. 43–56.

Hamlyn, D. W., 'Reply to David E. Cooper', *Journal of Philosophy of Education*, 14 (1980), pp. 105–8.

Hamlyn, D. W., *Schopenhauer* (Routledge & Kegan Paul, London, 1980).

Hamlyn, D. W., 'Cognitive systems, "folk psychology", and knowledge', *Cognition*, 10 (1981), pp. 115–18.

Hamlyn, D. W., 'Schopenhauer on action and the will' (1982), in *Idealism: Past and Present*, ed. G. N. A. Vesey (Cambridge University Press, Cambridge, 1982), pp. 127–40.

Hamlyn, D. W., 'The concept of social reality', in *Explaining Social Behavior*, ed. P. Secord (Sage Publications, Beverly Hills, London and New Delhi, 1982), pp. 189–209.

Hamlyn, D. W., 'What exactly is social about the origins of understanding?', in *Social Cognition*, ed. G. Butterworth and P. Light (Harvester, Brighton, 1982), pp. 17–31, also in *Perception, Learning and the Self*, pp. 162–77.

Hamlyn, D. W., 'Perception, information and attention' (1983), in *Perception, Learning and the Self*, pp. 57–68.

Hamlyn, D. W., *Perception, Learning and the Self* (Routledge & Kegan Paul, London, 1983).

Hamlyn, D. W., *Metaphysics* (Cambridge University Press, Cambridge, 1984).

Hamlyn, D. W., 'Motivation', in *Education, Values and Mind, Essays for R. S. Peters*, ed. D. E. Cooper (Routledge & Kegan Paul, London, 1986), pp. 188–200.

Hampshire, S. N., *Thought and Action* (Chatto & Windus, London, 1959).

Heil, J., 'Does cognitive psychology rest on a mistake?', *Mind*, 90 (1981), pp. 321–42.

Heil, J., *Perception and Cognition* (University of California Press, Berkeley, Los Angeles and London, 1983).

Held, R. and Hein, A., 'Movement-produced stimulation in the development of visually guided behavior', *Journal of Comparative Physiology*, 56 (1963), pp. 872–6.

Hopkins, J., 'Synthesis in the imagination, psychoanalysis, infantile experience and the concept of an object' (1987), in *Philosophical Perspectives on Developmental Psychology*, ed. J. Russell, pp. 140–72.

Hornsby, J., *Actions* (Routledge & Kegan Paul, London, 1980).

Humphreys, G. W. and Riddoch, M. J., 'Information processing systems which embody computational rules', *Mind and Language*, 1 (1986), pp. 201–12.

Humphreys, G. W. and Riddoch, M. J., *To See But Not To See* (Erlbaum, London, 1987).

Kant, I., *Critique of Pure Reason*, trans. N. Kemp Smith (Macmillan, London, 1929).

Kosslyn, S. M., *Image and Mind* (Harvard University Press, Cambridge, Mass., 1980).

McClelland, J. L., Rumelhart, D. E. and others, *Parallel Distributed Processing: Explorations in the Microstructure of Cognition* (2 vols, MIT Press, Cambridge, Mass., 1986).

Malcolm, N., 'The conceivability of mechanism', *Philosophical Review*, 77 (1968), pp. 45–72.

Malcolm, N., *Memory and Mind* (Cornell University Press, Ithaca, NY, 1977).

Manfredi, P. A., 'Processing or pickup: conflicting approaches to perception', *Mind and Language*, 1 (1986), pp. 181–200.

Marr, D., *Vision* (W. H. Freeman, San Francisco, 1982).

Marr, D. and Nishihara, H. K., 'Visual information processing: artificial intelligence and the sensorium of sight', *Technology Review*, October 1978, pp. 28–49.

Michotte, A., *La perception de la causalité* (Publications Universitaires de Louvain, Louvain, 2nd edn 1954).

Michotte, A., *Causalité, permanence et réalité phénoménales* (Publications Universitaires de Louvain, Louvain, 1962).

Millar, A., 'What's in a look?', *Proceedings of the Aristotelian Society*, 86 (1985/6), pp. 83–97.

Morgan, M. J., *Molyneux's Problem* (Cambridge University Press, Cambridge, 1977).

Neisser, U., *Cognition and Reality* (W. H. Freeman, San Francisco, 1976).

Nicholas, J. M. (ed.), *Images, Perception and Knowledge* (D. Reidel, Dordrecht, 1977).

O'Shaughnessy, B., *The Will* (2 vols, Cambridge University Press, Cambridge, 1980).

Paavio, A. V., 'Images, propositions and knowledge' (1977), in *Images, Perception and Knowledge*, ed. J. M. Nicholas, pp. 47–71.

Peacocke, C., *Holistic Explanation: Action, Space, Interpretation* (Clarendon Press, Oxford, 1979).

Peacocke, C., *Sense and Content* (Clarendon Press, Oxford, 1983).

Peacocke, C., *Thoughts: An Essay on Content* (Basil Blackwell, Oxford, 1986).

Piatelli-Palmarini, M., *Language and Learning: The Debate between Jean Piaget and Noam Chomsky* (Routledge & Kegan Paul, London, 1980).

Pitcher, G., *A Theory of Perception* (Princeton University Press, Princeton, NJ, 1971).

Plato, *Meno, Phaedo, Sophist, Theaetetus*.

Polanyi, M., *Personal Knowledge* (University of Chicago Press, Chicago, 1958).

Polanyi, M., *The Tacit Dimension* (Doubleday, New York, 1966).

Popper, K., *Objective Knowledge* (Clarendon Press, Oxford, 1972).

Pribram, K. H., 'Holonomy and structure in the organization of perception' (1977), in *Images, Perception and Knowledge*, ed. J. M. Nicholas, pp. 155–85.

Putnam, H., 'The meaning of "meaning"', in his *Mind, Language and Reality: Philosophical Papers*, vol. 2 (Cambridge University Press, Cambridge, 1975), pp. 215–71.

Pylyshyn, Z. W., *Computation and Cognition* (Bradford Books, MIT Press, Cambridge, Mass., 1984).

Quine, W. V., 'Two dogmas of empiricism', in his *From a Logical Point of View* (Harvard University Press, Cambridge, Mass., 1953).

Reid, T., *Essays on the Intellectual Powers of Man*, ed. A. D. Woozley (Macmillan, London and Basingstoke, 1941).

Rock, I., *The Nature of Perceptual Adaptation* (Basic Books Inc., New York and London, 1966).

Rorty, R., 'Mind–body identity, privacy and categories', *Review of Metaphysics*, 19 (1965), pp. 25–54, also in *The Philosophy of Mind*, ed. S. N. Hampshire (Harper & Row, New York, 1966).

Rorty, R., *Philosophy and the Mirror of Nature* (Basil Blackwell, Oxford, 1980).

Russell, B., *Problems of Philosophy* (Oxford University Press, London and Oxford, 1912).

Russell, B., 'The philosophy of logical atomism' (1918–19), in his *Logic and Knowledge*, ed. R. C. Marsh (Allen & Unwin, London, 1956).

Russell, J., *The Acquisition of Knowledge* (Macmillan, London and Basingstoke, 1978).

Russell, J., *Explaining Mental Life* (Macmillan, London and Basingstoke, 1984).

Russell, J. (ed.), *Philosophical Perspectives on Developmental Psychology* (Basil Blackwell, Oxford, 1987).

Russell, J., 'Reasons for retaining the view that there is perceptual development in childhood' (1987), in *Philosophical Perspectives on Developmental Psychology*, ed. J. Russell, pp. 81–115.

Ryle, G., *The Concept of Mind* (Hutchinson, London, 1949).

Ryle, G., 'Sensation', in *Contemporary British Philosophy, 3rd Series*, ed. H. D. Lewis (Allen & Unwin, London, 1956), pp. 427–43.

Scruton, R. V., *Art and Imagination* (Methuen, London, 1974).

Skinner, B. F., *The Behavior of Organisms* (Appleton-Century, New York, 1938).

Stich, S. P., 'Autonomous psychology and the belief–desire thesis', *The Monist*, 61 (1978), pp. 573–91.

Stich, S. P., *From Folk Psychology to Cognitive Science* (Bradford Books, MIT Press, Cambridge, Mass., 1983).

Strawson, P. F., 'Imagination and perception', in his *Freedom and Resentment* (Methuen, London, 1974), pp. 45–65.

Taylor, C., *The Explanation of Behaviour* (Routledge & Kegan Paul, London, 1964).

Treisman, A. M., 'Strategies and models of selective attention', *Psychological Review*, 76 (1969), pp. 282–99.

Von Senden, M., *Space and Sight*, trans. P. Heath (Methuen, London, 1960).

Ward, J., *Psychological Principles* (Cambridge University Press, Cambridge, 2nd edn 1920).

Watson, J. B., *Psychology from the Standpoint of a Behaviorist* (Lippincott, Philadelphia, 1919).

Watson, J. B., *Behaviorism* (Mouton, New York, 1925).

Weiskrantz, L., 'Trying to bridge the neuropsychological gap between monkey and man', *British Journal of Psychology*, 68 (1977), pp. 431–45.

Weiskrantz, L. and others, 'Visual capacity in the hemianopic field following a restricted ablation', *Brain*, 97 (1974), pp. 709–28.

Wittgenstein, L., *Philosophical Investigations* (Basil Blackwell, Oxford, 1953).

Woodfield, A., 'On the very idea of acquiring a concept' (1987), in *Philosophical Perspectives on Developmental Psychology*, ed. J. Russell, pp. 17–30.

Index